The Fabian Society

The Fabian Society is Britain's oldest political think tank. Since 1884 the society has played a central role in developing political ideas and public policy on the left.

Through a wide range of publications and events the society influences political and public thinking, but also provides a space for broad and open-minded debate, drawing on an unrivalled external network and its own expert research and analysis.

The society is alone among think tanks in being a democratically-constituted membership organisation, with more than 7,000 members. During its history the membership has included many of the key thinkers on the British left and every Labour prime minister. Today it counts over 200 parliamentarians in its number. Member-led activity includes 50 local Fabian societies, the Scottish and Welsh Fabians, the Fabian Women's Network and the Young Fabians, which is itself the leading organisation on the left for young people to debate and influence political ideas.

The society was one of the original founders of the Labour party and is constitutionally affiliated to the party. It is however editorially, organisationally and financially independent and works with a wide range of partners of all political persuasions and none.

www.fabians.org.uk

Joining the Fabians is easy
For more information about joining the Fabian Society please turn to the final page.

Foundation for European Progressive Studies

FEPS is the first progressive political foundation established at the European level. Created in 2007 and co-financed by the European Parliament, it aims at establishing an intellectual crossroad between social democracy and the European project. It puts fresh thinking at the core of its action and serves as an instrument for pan-European intellectual and political reflection.

Acting as a platform for ideas, FEPS relies first and foremost on a network of members composed of more than 58 national political foundations and think tanks from all over the EU. The Foundation also closely collaborates with a number of international correspondents and partners in the world that share the ambition to foster research, promote debate and spread the progressive thinking.

www.feps-europe.eu

You can also find FEPS on

 Facebook
 Twitter
 Netvibes

FOUNDATION FOR EUROPEAN
PROGRESSIVE STUDIES
FONDATION EUROPÉENNE
D'ÉTUDES PROGRESSISTES

BEYOND BREXIT

The left's agenda for the UK and EU

Edited by Olivia Bailey with a foreword by Keir Starmer QC MP.
With chapters by Stephen Bush, Richard Corbett MEP,
Sandro Gozi, Nia Griffiths MP, Stephany Griffiths Jones,
Jennifer Jackson-Preece, Maria Maltschnig, Lisa Nandy MP,
Kaisa Penny, Tomáš Petříček, Rachel Reeves MP, Nathalie Tocci
and Paola Sartori, Wes Streeting MP, Nick Thomas-Symonds MP.

FOUNDATION FOR EUROPEAN
PROGRESSIVE STUDIES
FONDATION EUROPÉENNE
D'ÉTUDES PROGRESSISTES

Fabian Society
61 Petty France
London SW1H 9EU
www.fabians.org.uk

Foundation for European Progressive Studies
Rue Montoyer 40
1000 Brussels, Belgium
www.feps-europe.eu

A FEPS/Fabian book
First published 2018
ISBN 978-0-7163-4131-4

Printed and bound by DG3
Designed and typeset by Soapbox, www.soapbox.co.uk
Cover image: lonndubh/Shutterstock.com

British Library Cataloguing in Publication data.
A catalogue record for this book is available from
the British Library.

CONTENTS

The rise of nationalism

A new political economy

Immigration and social integration

Bridging the generational divide

A path back?

CONTRIBUTORS

Olivia Bailey is deputy general secretary of the Fabian Society.

Stephen Bush is special correspondent for the *New Statesman*.

Richard Corbett is leader of the Labour party in the European parliament and member of the European parliament for Yorkshire and the Humber.

Sandro Gozi is a member of the Italian parliament representing the Democratic party. He was until recently a minister with responsibility for European affairs in the Italian government, and is currently senior advisor on EU affairs for the Democratic party.

Nia Griffiths is shadow defence secretary and the Labour member of parliament for Llanelli.

Professor Stephany Griffiths Jones is Financial Markets Program Director at the Initiative for Policy Dialogue at Columbia University. She is also a member of the scientific advisory council of FEPs and has advised the European Parliament and European Commission.

Jennifer Jackson-Preece is Associate Professor of Nationalism at the London School of Economics and Political Science. She is the project lead for Generation Brexit, which is crowdsourcing a pan-European millennial vision for the future of the UK/EU relationship.

Lisa Nandy is the Labour member of parliament for Wigan.

Kaisa Penny is director of the Kalevi Sorsa Foundation in Finland.

Tomáš Petříček is Deputy Minister of Foreign Affairs of the Czech Republic. He previously served as Deputy Minister of Social Affairs of the Czech Republic. He is a member of the Czech Social Democratic Party.

Rachel Reeves is the Labour member of parliament for Leeds West and chair of the business, energy and industrial strategy select committee.

Paola Sartori is research fellow in the Defence and Security programmes at the Italian Istituto Affari Internazionali (IAI).

Keir Starmer QC is the shadow secretary of state for exiting the EU and member of parliament for Holborn and St Pancras.

Wes Streeting is the Labour member of parliament for Ilford North and a member of the treasury select committee.

Nick Thomas-Symonds is shadow minister for security and the Labour member of parliament for Torfaen.

Nathalie Tocci is Director of the Italian Istituto Affari Internazionali (IAI) and Honorary Professor at the University of Tübingen.

Ernst Stetter is Secretary General of the Foundation for European Progressive Studies.

Andrew Harrop is General Secretary of the Fabian Society.

Maria Maltschnig is director of the Renner Institute in Austria.

PREFACE

Ernst Stetter and Andrew Harrop

Britain's decision in the 2016 EU referendum was a shock for progressives in the UK and across the EU. In the context of serious social and economic challenges, cynical but persuasive and optimistic arguments for leaving triumphed over a cautious remain campaign that seemed only to offer the prospect of risk.

Since the result, debate on the left hasn't got much broader. We have spent most of our time preoccupied with the detail of the negotiations. Now the question of a second referendum is dominating to the exclusion of debate on the post Brexit future.

We both wish that the UK was remaining in the EU, and another referendum may well be the right course of action to break the stalemate in the negotiations. But the UK's departure from the EU next March is still much more likely than a second vote. And even if there is a second referendum, we are still no closer to understanding how the remain message can win. Whether we like it or not, we need to prepare for Brexit.

Our objective for this book is to bring together key opinion formers from the UK and the rest of Europe to try to broaden the conversation about Brexit. We asked authors to put aside short term considerations, and try and imagine the UK and EU after Brexit has actually happened.

The essays make a compelling case for close collaboration between the UK and EU, and sketch out the start of an agenda for helping the left deal with the social and economic drivers of Brexit after the UK has left the EU. We hope that they encourage further conversation across Europe.

There is an adage which says "when nothing is clear, anything is possible." That is the spirit which the left should embody as it faces a future after Brexit. If the left has the courage to do so, it can win the support of the public for a close relationship between the UK and the EU and start to build a compelling programme to tackle our shared social and economic challenges.

FOREWORD

Keir Starmer

Brexit is more than a technical process. If the left is to succeed in decisively shaping the decades to come, a strong Brexit deal must come alongside a compelling vision for the future and a radical social and economic programme.

More than two years on from the referendum, Brexit remains the central issue in British politics. Barely a day goes by when Brexit is not the lead, or among the lead, news stories. Parliament, otherwise devoid of legislation, is dominated by Brexit bills. It is the top issue for every government department. And polling consistently shows that voters believe Brexit is the most important issue facing the country.[1]

Yet while there has been no shortage of coverage and commentary on Brexit, too often the debate has been narrow, technical and insular. Countless hours have been spent arguing over the technicalities of the single market, the customs union, the European Economic Area or the European Court of Justice.

A new and largely impenetrable language (*Brexitspeak* perhaps?) has emerged, packed with terms such as 'regulatory alignment', 'managed divergence', 'facilitated customs arrangements', 'association agreements' and 'reciprocal non-regression commitments'.

But what has gripped the attention of politicians and commentators in Westminster is failing to cut through with the public. The language of Brexit no longer resonates with voters. And the issues that gave rise to the referendum result – in particular a growing feeling among many people that our political and economic system no longer works for them or their families – remain unaddressed. No wonder a majority of people now say they are "really bored" by Brexit.[2]

When I campaigned for remain in 2016, few people wanted to talk about the technicalities of the customs union or the single market. People wanted to talk about the problems with their local hospital, the difficulties they had buying a home, how they hadn't had a pay rise for years, or how they were increasingly frustrated with an immigration system they felt simply didn't work for their community.

For many, the response was to vote to leave the EU. They wanted change. And they were not alone; many who voted remain also wanted to see radical and fundamental change to the way our country and our economy works. It may well be that many of these problems have little, if anything, to do with our relationship with the EU. But they were exposed by the referendum, and they need to be addressed.

Yet in the months that have followed the referendum this cry for change has been drowned out. The focus has been instead on the deal with the EU; the technicalities of our future relationship. Should we remain very close – particularly economically – with the EU and continue to cooperate in a wide range of areas? Or should we have a more distant, arms-length relationship, perhaps even departing without a deal?

These are hugely important questions, which warrant careful thought and robust scrutiny. So many aspects of our lives depend on the answers to these questions, and that is why Labour has fought so hard for a future relationship with the EU that keeps us close and is rooted in our core values and principles. It is also why we have been clear that an abrupt rupture with the EU, or leaving with no deal, would be catastrophic.

But there is another side to the Brexit debate. Not just the deal with the EU but also the need for a fairer, more equal and transformed Britain.

It is a source of huge frustration to me that we have been unable to move this aspect of the debate forward or to talk about the wider questions arising from Brexit – from funding our public services, protecting our environment and safeguarding human rights, to the nature of our future defence and security policy. It is these issues that I believe need much greater attention, because there can be no satisfactory response to the referendum unless the right deal with the EU is accompanied by a new deal for Britain.

For the left in British politics, Brexit also poses a particular problem. Frankly, few of us ever thought we would need to consider what a future outside the EU looks like. Certainly when I became an MP in 2015, I never thought for a second that this would become the defining issue of our time. Among all the heated debates the Labour party and the wider labour movement has had over many years, Europe rarely featured.

Consequently, there is now an urgent need for renewed thought, debate and discussion on the left. Not just about how we reshape our relationship with the EU, but about how we bring about the wider change our country needs.

That discussion needs to consider what the building blocks should be for a strong new relationship with the EU that can protect jobs, rights and our security. It needs to reimagine how we build an economy properly to fund public services and invest in the country's infrastructure. How we work with our allies across the world to respond to the huge challenges of the century – from climate change to terrorism. And how progressive, social democratic values can bring a divided country back together after so many years of Tory misrule.

This is no small task. Yet asking these questions and seeking to provide these answers will be central to any future left platform in the years and decades to come. That is why this collection of essays is so welcome.

The collection considers the questions that have too often been ignored and marginalised – from the future of our defence and foreign policy, to how we can reform our economy and immigration system to reflect core Labour values.

Over the last two years Labour has made the case for a close future partnership with the EU and a Brexit deal that is rooted in our core values and principles. Our policy will of course continue to evolve and develop. But we must also remind ourselves that whatever the ups and downs of the negotiations, Brexit is more than a technical process – and that if the Left is to succeed in decisively shaping the decades to come, a strong Brexit deal must come alongside a compelling vision for the future and a radical social and economic programme.

---

1   YouGov tracker poll shows Brexit is the no 1 issue of concern for voters throughout 2018: https://d25d2506sfb94s.cloudfront.net/cumulus_uploads/document/yvvp1agvnp/YG%20Trackers%20-%20Top%20Issues_W.pdf

2   www.deltapoll.co.uk/wp-content/uploads/2018/08/SOS-website-post.pdf (59%).

INTRODUCTION: SPACE FOR LEADERSHIP
Olivia Bailey

If Labour can break free of its tactical stasis, new polling for this collection shows there is space for it to lead. This leadership should not be confined to the question of a second referendum. The left can win public support for a close working relationship with the EU after Brexit, and for a radical domestic programme to tackle the drivers of Brexit.

Brexit has dominated the news agenda for more than two years. We have debated every possible technicality in the negotiations, gasped at the Tory Brexit psychodrama and started to wonder if we should just run the whole vote again.

The left in Britain has weathered these two stormy years in a tactical pose. Pragmatism and moderation have rightly triumphed. But the unintended consequence of too much time spent discussing the negotiations has been too little time thinking about the bigger picture. In his foreword to this collection, Keir Starmer accepts that this is a 'source of great frustration'.

At the heart of the left's challenge sit the social and economic drivers of Brexit. Politicians know what they are, but do not yet know how to address them outside of the EU. There has also been insufficient thought on how the UK and the EU can work together after Brexit. These questions are the focus of this book.

None of the UK politicians who have contributed essays supported Brexit. Some are perhaps still hoping it won't happen. But for this project they have been willing to look beyond the technicalities of the negotiations to consider the UK's post Brexit future. The EU contributions offer useful perspectives on the challenges faced by the EU in the same period.

To help root this conversation in the reality of public opinion, we commissioned a new survey of public attitudes on Britain's post Brexit future.[1] Our findings reveal that there is space for leadership from the left. Despite the continued potency of the leave campaign's messages, we find no support for a 'no deal' Brexit and little evidence that people believe the benefits of Brexit will grow in the long term. We also find a strong sense that the UK has a lot in common with its European neighbours, and a very pragmatic approach to our future relationship with the EU.

If progressives can develop the 'radical social and economic programme' that Keir Starmer calls for, as well as make a compelling case for working closely with the EU, there is no reason to believe that they won't be able to take the public with them.

No belief in long-term benefit

Jacob Rees Mogg recently argued that the UK might have to wait a generation to see the benefits of Brexit, but our survey suggests that the public do not share his optimism. Working with YouGov, we developed an experiment to compare people's expectations for Brexit over the short and long term. We asked one sample of the public to tell us whether they felt Brexit would have a positive or negative impact on a range of issues in five years time (by 2024), and a different sample the same questions but considering the impact 25 years after Brexit (by 2044). We found there was very little difference between short term and long term expectations, suggesting that very few people believe that short term pain will lead to long term gain. On the issues we examined, the long term 'sunlit uplands' perspective yields no more optimism than the near term view.

Figure 1: Percentage of GB adults who said they expected Brexit to have a positive impact in each area by 2024 or 2044

	2024	2044	Positivity bounce?
Workers' rights	23	22	-1
Jobs	29	33	+4
Prices	14	16	+2
Business investment in Britain	28	29	+1
Immigration	42	41	-1
Security and terrorism	29	32	+3
Control over laws	59	59	0
UK influence in world	28	29	+1
Equality	18	21	+3
The environment	19	20	+1
Public services in Britain	28	28	0
Pride in Britain	45	44	-1

The margin of error for the results from the two samples is +/- 3 per cent, so there is only one statistically significant difference between the 2024 and 2044 groups. This relates to positivity about jobs. Four per cent more people felt that Brexit would have a positive impact by 2044. However, only a third (33 per cent) of the public said there will be positive impact on jobs at all, and this is still behind the proportion of the public who believe there will be a negative impact (35 per cent).

No desire for a 'no deal' Brexit

Our survey also reveals that almost no one wants a Brexit that leads to a bitter and antagonistic relationship with the EU. This indicates that there is no appetite for a 'no deal' Brexit. We asked people to imagine that the negotiations were over and tell us what kind of relationship they think the UK should have with the EU. Strikingly, only 4 per cent of the population said that they want a 'distant and cold' relationship with the EU, which most would say is the inevitable consequence of crashing out of the Union without reaching agreement. Leave voters were no more likely to want a distant relationship with the EU than remain voters.

Figure 2: Imagine the negotiations are over and the UK has left the EU. Which statement best describes how you'd like to see the UK's relationship with the EU? (%)

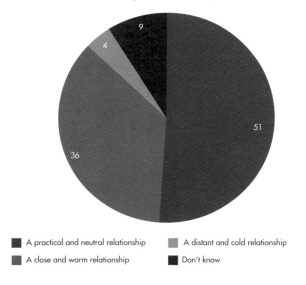

■ A practical and neutral relationship   ■ A distant and cold relationship
■ A close and warm relationship   ■ Don't know

Over half of those surveyed (51 per cent) said that they'd like a 'practical and neutral' relationship with the EU after Brexit, suggesting that pragmatism is the dominant consideration for the public. This pragmatism was popular among remain voters too, with a third of them (33 per cent) selecting a 'practical and neutral' relationship over a 'close and warm' relationship (57 per cent).

Leave messages are still potent and persuasive

Another key finding is that the core messages from the leave campaign are still potent and persuasive, and people still have confidence that they will be delivered. We asked

Figure 3: Which two or three things do you think politicians should be prioritising as we prepare to leave the EU? Please tick up to three (%)

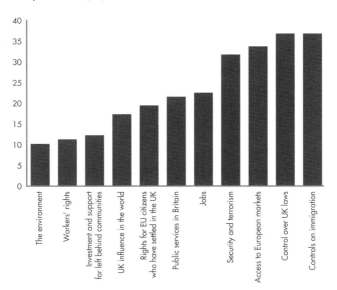

people to think about Britain after Brexit, and asked them what politicians should be prioritising as we prepare to leave. As figure three shows, the most popular issues were control over UK laws and controls on immigration.

These issues remain potent because they are the public's top priorities for Brexit, but also because they are the issues where most people believe Brexit will deliver benefits. On control of laws, 59 per cent think that Brexit will have had a positive impact by 2044. This figure is also high amongst Labour voters, with nearly half (47 per cent)

Figure 4: Percentage who selected 'positive impact' minus percentage who selected 'negative impact'

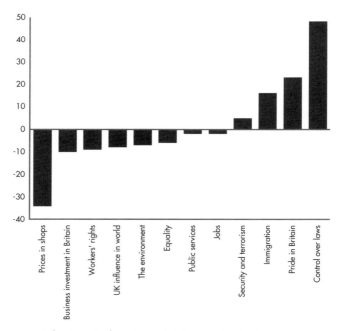

Note: a significant proportion for each issue selected 'no impact' or 'don't know'.

saying the impact will be positive. On the broader patriotic issue of 'pride in Britain', 44 per cent say that Brexit will have had a positive impact by 2044. 41 per cent think the impact will be positive on immigration. And, as figure four shows, the net positivity ratings for these three issues were the highest.

The graph also reveals that the majority of issues we tested received a negative net positivity rating. This is particularly stark on the question of prices in shops. But this doesn't necessarily spell good news for remainers: the experience of the referendum showed that messages based on risk were not as effective as optimistic messages that promised something better.

People don't feel European, but do recognise commonalities

We asked people about their connection to their European identity, and a majority (52 per cent) said that they don't currently feel European. This figure was also high amongst Labour voters (40 per cent) and remain voters (30 per cent). It shouldn't surprise us that such a high proportion of people don't feel an emotional identification with Europe; had we felt European as a country, EU membership probably wouldn't have been up for debate.

But our poll also reveals a surprising sense of commonality with other European countries. 61 per cent of those surveyed said that they think we have a lot in common with our European neighbours. This is also the case for the majority of leave voters (52 per cent). Our results suggest that practical messages about maintaining links with other European countries will be much more effective than emotional appeals based on shared European identity.

We also explored to what extent people feel that leaving the European Union will affect their European identity and their perceptions of the UK's commonalities with Europe.

On both questions, opinion is divided. 13 per cent say that they expect to feel less European after Brexit, whereas the other 22 per cent of people who currently feel European don't feel like Brexit will have an impact. 33 per cent feel we have a lot in common with other European countries and don't feel this will change as a result of Brexit, while 28 per cent expect commonalities will decline over time.

Figure 5: Commonalities with other European countries (%)

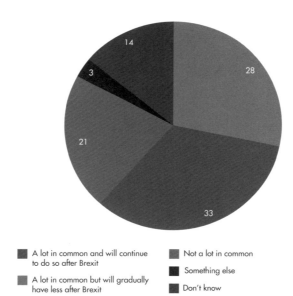

A lot in common and will continue to do so after Brexit

A lot in common but will gradually have less after Brexit

Not a lot in common

Something else

Don't know

The country remains deeply divided

Our survey confirms how divided the UK has become. Across all the questions, there is evidence of continued polarisation of views between leave and remain voters. On every issue we tested, more leave voters said the impacts of Brexit would be positive than negative, and more remain voters said the impacts would be negative rather than positive. The only exception to this for remain voters was control over laws, which slightly more remain voters believed would be a positive consequence of Brexit.

We can also see the demographic divides that were so evident in the referendum result itself. One of the most pronounced is the age divide. Two thirds of over 65s (67 per cent) said that they don't currently feel European, compared to just 34 per cent of 18–24 year olds. Young people are also less enthusiastic about core leave messages, with 18–24 year olds 37 points less likely to select 'control over laws' as a priority for politicians than the over 65s.

There are also clear geographic splits. Key findings from our polling include that people in the North are 10 points more likely to think Brexit will be good for jobs than people in London, and 14 points more likely to think Brexit will be good for public services. People in London are also more likely to feel as though they have something in common with other European countries. 71 per cent of Londoners say Britain has a lot in common with other European countries, compared to 58 per cent of people in the North and 56 per cent of people in the Midlands and Wales.

We also know that social class was an important factor in the referendum result. People who were less well off were more likely to be leave voters, and this had important intersections with levels of education. Our survey suggests this divide continues to be pertinent with working class people less likely to feel European, less likely to say the UK has commonalities with Europe and more likely to select core leave issues as key priorities for politicians.[2]

Facing a future beyond Brexit

These findings give the left some cause for optimism. There is no appetite for an antagonistic 'no deal' Brexit and little confidence that Brexit will be better for Britain in 25 years time than in 5 years time. The majority of people in this country recognise how much we have in common with our European neighbours, and have a pragmatic approach to our future relationship with the EU. But the findings also underline the scale of the challenge. Two years after the referendum, leave messages are still very effective, and we are no closer to bringing our divided country back together.

If Labour can break free of its tactical stasis, there is space for it to lead. This leadership should not just be confined to the question of a second referendum, which is currently dominating the conversation on the left. It should also be about building public support for a close working relationship with the EU after Brexit, and for a radical domestic programme to tackle the drivers of Brexit. It would be negligent to ignore the prospect of our future after Brexit just because we are hoping that another referendum might make the problem go away.

The essays in this collection reveal the outline of a progressive prospectus to rival the potency of the leave campaign's messages. Rachel Reeves argues we need a new political economy rooted in people's everyday lives. Wes Streeting contends that we must bring our country back together around a politics that is patriotic, democratic and open to the world. Nia Griffiths sets out a framework for the UK's revived role on the world stage, and Lisa Nandy argues that we must give people more control over their own lives and communities.

The essays are also honest about the UK's future relationship with the EU, and about the challenges we face. Richard Corbett argues we have to accept that there are no half measures in the negotiations. Nick Thomas-Symonds, exploring the question of security cooperation, exposes just how important a close continued relationship with the EU will be. Jennifer Jackson Preece's essay on the generational divide is a reminder that the generation most affected by Brexit is the generation who wanted it least. The essays from our EU contributors give a flavour of how the EU will fare without the UK, and demonstrate that partnership is the best way to face up to our shared challenges.

Stephen Bush concludes by arguing that the UK is likely to seek to return to the EU in the future. Only time will tell if he is right, but what is clear is that the future is there for the pro-European left to grasp. Britain's decision to leave the EU was a consequence of progressives' failure. The challenge now is to build a compelling offer which addresses the root causes of Brexit and which makes the case for a close relationship with our European neighbours.

---

1 The results are analysed in full on the Fabian Society website. All figures, unless otherwise stated, are from YouGov Plc. Total sample size was 1,660 adults. Fieldwork was undertaken between 13–14 August 2018. The question on positives and negatives in 2044 was run on the 16–17 August with a sample size of 1676. Both surveys were carried out online. The figures have been weighted and are representative of all GB adults (aged 18+).

2 Working class is defined here as people in social grades C2DE.

1 | HALF MEASURES WON'T WORK

Richard Corbett

The government has backed itself in to a corner on Brexit. But it's time to accept that half measures won't work when it comes to negotiating our future relationship with the EU.

The central dilemma of Brexit boils down to a battle between sovereignty and market access. The more the UK disengages itself from the workings of the European Union, its single market and its customs union, the less it can trade with the EU and, therefore, the greater the economic damage. But if the UK remains close to the EU, in a model not dissimilar to the Norway arrangement, many have pointed out that we would have to abide by the rules, without having much of a say on them.

Neither scenario seems good for Britain. But let us look at that second option. It is what the government is slowly staggering towards, as it finally dawns on senior Conservative politicians that the other option entails huge economic costs. Not to mention that it would be impossible to avoid a hard border in Northern Ireland without regulatory alignment on goods and staying in an effective customs union. A close relationship with the single market is also what the Labour Party, trade unions, and most businesses consider to be the lesser of two evils.

But how would such a relationship work after Brexit and what are the practical trade-offs that would have to take place to make it happen? As the past eighteen months of negotiations have shown time and time again, half measures do not work. As a country we are facing some tough choices if we want to go for a close working relationship with the EU and avoid a disastrous "no-deal" outcome.

No horse trading

The first choice facing the government is on trade in goods and services. In its long-delayed white paper, the government proposed a 'common rulebook' on goods wherever necessary to maintain frictionless trade at the Irish border. In practice, this means following the EU rulebook. But on services, the white paper seeks to diverge from EU rules, and therefore shut itself out of a single market for services. This amounts to shooting ourselves in our stronger foot, since we have a trade surplus in services with the EU and EFTA countries, exporting £106 billion in 2016 alone, and services make up 80 per cent of economic activity in the UK.

But this proposal also won't fly with the rest of the EU. Increasingly, goods and services are intertwined in international trade. This is because the sale of goods is often linked to corresponding services, such as post-sale maintenance, purchasing loans, marketing or accounting. Trade experts estimate that these embedded services are worth more than £50 billion in UK exports every year.

Separating goods and services also clashes with the EU's commitment to the four freedoms. Although the EU might allow for some flexibility further down the line, it is anxious to avoid separating these and it will not be easy for the UK to pick and choose some and not others. The EU will be further concerned that a future deregulated services sector in the UK could give British manufacturers an unfair advantage over their neighbours, while increasing the risk factor for financial stability.

For all these reasons, the choice is not between goods or services. The UK can participate in the market for both, or for neither.

The same dilemma for security

A similar choice looms on security cooperation. Outside the EU, the UK could lose access to shared systems such as the European Arrest Warrant, which facilitates the quick extradition of criminals from one EU country to another. Europol and the Schengen Information System are also important tools.

The European Arrest Warrant is not a CIA-style rendition system. It comes with the safeguards of the EU's legal eco-system, not least the Charter of Fundamental Rights and the right to appeal on points of law to the European Court of Justice (ECJ). To the chagrin of many of her backbenchers, and contrary to her previous statements, Theresa May has now indicated through her white paper that the UK would on occasion refer to ECJ case law after Brexit. But even if this promise sticks, the government has already legislated itself out of the Charter of Fundamental Rights through the EU (Withdrawal) Act. Having belatedly declared the importance of mechanisms like the European Arrest Warrant for public safety, the government will need to cross even more of its red lines to build a strong relationship with the EU on security.

Arbitration, dispute settlement and sovereignty: not so simple

The influence of the European Court of Justice is also at the heart of discussions around future dispute settlements with the rest of the EU. As in any international agreement, mechanisms need to be put in place in case one of the parties reneges on their commitments, or simply to settle divergent interpretations of texts that have been agreed. The government's white paper suggests that the UK and the EU create a joint committee that monitors compliance and resolves disputes, with an independent arbitration panel to step in where the committee does not reach agreement. This sounds simple enough, but would require an enormous amount of resources, money and responsibility to stay functional – and even then would likely lack the teeth needed to function effectively.

It is worth looking at the sorts of agreements that govern similar relationships with close partners to the EU. Much has already been said about the Norway and Swiss models, but what do they actually mean in practice?

Switzerland is tied to the EU through more than 120 bilateral agreements that are governed by joint committees. But without a court to interpret these agreements, disputes between the two parties can go on for years without resolution. The EU has already strongly indicated that it will not replicate the bilateral Swiss system with the UK, and the UK would be wise to avoid it anyway.

Meanwhile, Norway, part of the European Economic Area, has more than 130 agreements with the EU. Norway is part of an EEA joint committee that decides which new EU laws will be incorporated into EEA law. It is also signed up to the EFTA Surveillance Authority (ESA) and the EFTA court, which respectively monitor compliance and deliver judgments on EEA law. Norway does not formally acknowledge the supremacy of EU or EEA law, but in practice through its referrals to ECJ case law, the EFTA court follows the rulings of the ECJ closely. If the UK were to dock into the EFTA court (or anything like it), it would need to be willing to accept ECJ rulings.

Curiously, the government has indicated that its joint committees would defer to ECJ rulings on matters related to the 'common rulebook', thereby giving the UK less of a say on the single market in goods than the EEA countries. This decision sparked much of the ire of Tory backbenchers, but even if it is extended to services as well, it is difficult to see how the EU will sign up to the dispute resolution mechanisms envisaged in the white paper.

All of which returns us to a debate about sovereignty. Leading Brexit supporters in the Tory party claim that leaving the EU, the customs union and the single market will allow us to 'take back control of our money, borders, law and trade'. But whichever way you spin Brexit, the UK will actually lessen its control of these four prized indicators of sovereignty.

Take money. Britain's net contribution to the EU, less than 1 per cent of public spending, will be dramatically overshadowed by the costs of Brexit, especially if the government continues with its plan to take the UK out of the single market for services.

Our border controls will be less effective if we drop out of the Schengen Information System, Europol and the EU's 'Dublin' regulations that allow Britain to send asylum seekers back to the first EU country they entered.

On trade, there is the still underestimated problem of dropping out of all the EU's existing agreements with countries across the world and replacing them with our own separate agreements. Simultaneously, and in a hurry, we will have to negotiate these without the clout of the EU, the world's largest market, behind us.

And, on control of our laws, UK businesses will still have to follow EU rules so they can continue selling into their single largest market. This will be the case even with a loose Canada style agreement on trade. The ability to have some influence over those rules from outside the EU, even with an EEA type agreement, will be far less than we have as a member state.

After ruling out a Canada style agreement because it would cause a hard border in Northern Ireland, and crossing off a Norway style model because of their red lines, the Tories have backed themselves into a corner on Brexit. It's the Chequers deal or nothing. The 'no-deal' rhetoric has ramped up over the summer because the government simply cannot figure out how to reach an arrangement with the rest of the EU that will (a) sufficiently water down the Chequers deal and (b) keep the conservative party together.

Something has to give

There is an alternative that could be explored, though it would probably need a different government. The UK could negotiate a new deal with the single market that includes both goods and services, form a customs union with the EU, and accept the judicial oversight of an international court as well as a monitoring system very similar to the EFTA surveillance authority. We would also have to invest heavily in the capacity of the foreign office, and accept that we will have to follow rules with less of a say than before.

It can be done, but people are already questioning whether this 'lesser of two evils' is really worth Brexit at all. It is certainly a far cry from the sunlit uplands promised by the leave campaigners. No wonder opinion seems to be shifting against Brexit itself.

2 | A POSITIVE VISION FOR OUR ROLE IN THE WORLD

Nia Griffiths

After Brexit the UK must step up and use our not inconsiderable influence on the world stage. This includes developing a positive vision for the future of defence, and building the UK's role in supporting conflict resolution and post conflict work.

There is significant alignment between the UK and the EU on defence and security cooperation after Brexit. Our interests overlap significantly and it is unlikely that will change in the near future, given an increasingly assertive Russia and the continued threat of terrorism.

There are, of course, points of contention and, naturally, complications in working out a new relationship. But the general approach, from both sides, about future defence and security cooperation is positive. The structure is also there to deliver it. NATO has long worked with the EU to ensure that its work and the defence work of the EU are complimentary.

Our defence relationships with individual European partners will remain close. The overlap between EU and NATO memberships is significant, and the bilateral and multilateral relationships we have with European partners are strong and expanding. The combined joint expeditionary force with France and the work of our marines with their Dutch counterparts as part of the UK-Netherlands amphibious force are just some examples. In many meaningful ways, things will remain unchanged after Brexit.

But it also true that we find ourselves at a crossroads; both for the UK's role on the world stage, and for defence policy. The Labour party must look to provide some answers.

It's been over a year since the government announced a root and branch national security capability review. Initially this included defence but the Ministry of Defence (MoD) element was hived off in January into a separate review, the modernising defence programme (MDP). The results of the MDP cannot simply be crisis management. We need a positive vision for the future, driven by our defence and security needs and not by the Treasury.

Of course, it is important to have discipline in the MoD about how much money you have, what you spend it on and how that impacts outside your department. The MDP should look at reversing some of the changes made in the recent Levene reforms to have a more strategic, centralised budgetary approach, or at least set out a new vision about how the department maintains a grip.

The structure of the forces must support the tasks they've been asked to do, ensure there are enough personnel to deliver and that there is the right balance of experience at various levels. The MDP should examine good practice examples of services working collaboratively and it should aim to promote joint working. The creation of the Joint Forces Command has been a success and its impact should be maximised.

In reality, it is almost unthinkable that the UK would ever deploy a significant force outside of a larger coalition. It is important that we shape the armed forces as such; to be interoperable with our NATO allies, and to maximise what we do well whilst being aware of our allies' strengths.

One area where we must continue to lead is the development and manufacture of cutting edge defence technology. We are the second largest defence exporter in the world, with an annual turnover of £22 billion and 140,000 direct employees, many of whom are highly skilled and well-paid. It is an important contributor to the national economy and very significant to local economies. Furthermore, having onshore defence industrial capacity is not only good for the economy it is also good for our security.

This is why it is so important that these industries are able to continue to thrive post Brexit and why the government must give them more certainty. The defence sector has extensive supply chains and it is vital that supplies are able to flow easily across borders, so a customs union is the only answer.

But outside of Brexit policy, the government is failing to take action and change how we procure our defence equipment to support the industry. At present, the MoD does not factor in the socioeconomic value of defence contracts when they are making procurement decisions. This means that the many benefits of awarding work in Britain go unaccounted for. These include the additional revenue that comes back to the Exchequer in taxation, higher national insurance contributions and lower social security payments. Not to mention the value of apprenticeships and spending in the wider economy.

Overall, there is a lack of a holistic, comprehensive plan when it comes to how we procure defence equipment and this needs to be changed. That's why labour is committed to a defence industrial strategy to have a clear vision of what we are procuring and a definition of good value that looks at how the defence pound impacts on our economy and employment.

Labour's defence industrial strategy would encourage research and development, and promote links with universities. There should also be the promotion of design for export and we must work in collaboration with allies to develop new assets, ensuring that there is a good amount of work for the UK. This is more important than ever in the context of Brexit and the need to forge strong trading relationships.

However, it is also important that trade is done in a responsible way that aligns with our values. Arms export controls have been eroded under both the coalition and Conservative governments, and we must ensure that the arms trade treaty is upheld to a consistently high standard.

After Brexit, the UK must step up and use our not inconsiderable influence on the world stage. We face a great deal of uncertainty, not only in relation to Brexit, but in the wider global environment. Threats are changing, global dynamics are shifting, and the world is becoming more and more interconnected. Britain must use its defence, diplomacy and development policies in harmony to deal with rising challenges. That is what Labour must offer in government. A strategic, focused approach to foreign affairs driven by the values that we share: respect for human rights, the rule of law and equality. We must not shy away from making tough decisions or being critical, even to our friends, where needed.

As part of this, I believe that there is an opportunity, and a need, to take a lead on UN peacekeeping efforts. This is driven by the desire to have our defence policy support our overall foreign policy aims, as outlined by Jeremy Corbyn, of "solidarity, calm leadership and cooperation".

The UN has been clear that the five permanent members of the security council (P5) are crucial to drive forward peacekeeping. It is important that the P5 are willing to make substantive contributions. The Santos Cruz report, a high level report on UN peacekeeping, clearly highlighted that a deficit of leadership is one of the main problems that prevents the United Nations from adapting, and under a Labour government the UK would step up and take that leadership role.

Our armed forces have valuable skills to offer in areas identified by the UN as needing uplift, such as engineering and medical skills, tactical airlift and an expertise in training other troops, to name but a few.

A Labour government would also look at how the UN and the structures within it can take better advantage of the offers made by states of troop and equipment contributions quickly and efficiently. This would not be focused on making large sweeping changes but small substantive alterations to structure that make an impact.

For the avoidance of doubt, a refocus and recommitment to peacekeeping does not mean we are ignoring the security of the UK and our citizens. Far from it. What we have learned from recent history is that bad things happen in ungoverned spaces. Where there is a void, someone will fill it, and sometimes those who fill it want to harm the UK, its interests and our citizens. The security of the UK is significantly enhanced by the stability and prosperity of states across the world.

We have an opportunity to return to the spirit of defence diplomacy that the Labour government set out in the 1998 strategic defence review; linking defence policy, foreign policy and international development in order to have the biggest impact.

Labour is ambitious about the UK's defence capabilities and ambitious about the UK's role in supporting conflict resolution and post-conflict work. Defence is not an area that the left should shy away from beyond Brexit, but rather an area where there are challenges to rise to, in order to make a positive impact on global peace and security.

3 | DEEPENING OUR SECURITY CO-OPERATION

Nick Thomas-Symonds

The UK must maintain and deepen its close security co-operation with the EU after Brexit. Despite their warm words, the government has no credible plan to make this happen. This reveals a reckless attitude towards UK security.

I n a digital age where crime knows no borders, it is critical that the United Kingdom's security policy enables its authorities to co-operate with speed and efficiency with its international partners. Not only do we need to maintain our close security co-operation with our European neighbours, we also need to have the means to deepen it as necessary as threats evolve in years to come.

Until the end of March 2019, we have at our disposal a toolkit of legislative powers and resources that allow us to work effectively with our fellow European Union member states, but what does the future hold for the UK's security after our withdrawal from the EU? Few people doubt the value of continuing to work together closely, but the government has produced no credible plan as to how the current advantages will continue post-Brexit. The lack of such a plan is evidence of a reckless attitude towards UK security.

The prime minister, in her speech at the Munich security conference on 17 February 2018, indicated that the

13

government will seek a security treaty with the twenty-seven remaining members of the EU. Yet she has provided no detail as to the planned architecture of security co-operation. At present, as a full EU member, the UK enjoys the benefits of the European Arrest Warrant (EAW), Eurojust and Europol, all of which are critical to the successful investigation and extradition of wanted suspects or criminals.

The European Arrest Warrant

As an arrest warrant valid throughout all the member states of the EU, an EAW, once issued, compels other member states to arrest and extradite wanted criminals or suspects from one to another to face trial, or complete a prison sentence. According to the National Crime Agency's statistics, between 2010 and 2016, the UK issued 1,773 requests to member states for extradition under the EAW and received 48,776 requests from member states for extradition. 11 of the requests submitted by UK were for terror offences, 71 relating to human trafficking, 206 relating to child sex offences and 255 to drug trafficking.[1] Not only can the UK bring people to these shores to face justice, the country is also able to send potentially dangerous people in our midst to other countries to face legal proceedings there.

In their white paper published in July 2018 the government accepts the importance of this tool, setting out that the UK has arrested *"more than 12,000 individuals, and for every person arrested on an EAW issued by the UK, the UK arrests eight on EAWs issued by other member states."* Yet the white paper also stresses the difficulty the government now finds itself in, noting that other arrangements between the EU and third countries do not provide the 'same level of capability' as the EAW. It goes on to add that being a third country creates 'challenges' for full cooperation with the EAW due to 'constitutional barriers in some member states'.[2]

Identification of a problem is something, but the government's failure to offer any sort of long-term solution is reckless. The government's thinking has not moved beyond the implementation period. In June 2018, Nick Hurd MP, the minister of state for the Home Office, responded to a written question submitted by shadow Brexit minister Paul Blomfield in time-limited terms: *"The draft agreement reached with the European Commission in March means police and criminal justice cooperation, including using the European Arrest Warrant, with the EU and its Member States can continue through the implementation period to December 2020."*[3] The July 2018 white paper only promises that these transitional arrangements *"should be the basis for the future relationship on extradition"*.[4] This is simply not good enough.

The wider eco-system

In her speech to the Commons on 5 March 2018, Theresa May cited security as one of the five tests by which she would weigh the value of our deal with the European Union.[5] Yet, as a third country, the UK cannot simply "opt-in" to the existing infrastructure for security co-operation. The EU has made its view on this plain. As the EU's Chief Negotiator on Brexit, Michel Barnier, has stated: *"If you leave this "ecosystem", you lose the benefits of this cooperation. You are a third country because you have decided to be so. And you need to build a new relationship."*[6]

The eco-system is made up of more than the EAW. There is Eurojust, created to improve the handling of serious cross-border and organised crime by stimulating investigative and prosecutorial cooperation, and supporting judicial cooperation. There is also Europol and the Schengen Information System (SIS) which offer critical support when executing international, time-sensitive operations by pooling data from across the EU and from its Schengen Partners. Such a loss of a resource could produce manifold issues, including delays in gathering evidence from other countries.[7]

Further to this, the cross-party House of Lords European Union committee emphasised the necessity of data-sharing between the EU and UK in their report published in July 2018. When outlining its findings, the committee echoed concerns raised that there is a lack of a long-term solution in place after the transition period ends to minimise any impact on the data-sharing to serve security purposes post-Brexit: *"continued data-sharing is critical for future UK-EU security cooperation. Were the UK to lose access to the EU's security databases, information that today can be retrieved almost instantaneously could take days or weeks to access, creating not only a significant hurdle to effective policing but a threat to public safety."*[8]

The future relationship

In the first instance, the government needs to emphasise the UK's contribution and be more ambitious about a treaty that moves beyond any other similar one in place. The third-party relationship offered by the deal struck with both Norway and Iceland has been considered as a possible model for a future EU-UK security relationship. Brokered in 2006 and still not successfully implemented, this model makes provision for the expedited extradition of wanted individuals along the lines of the EAW, but with significant problems including additional grounds for refusal to surrender.

The UK contribution to EU Security is highly significant. One example that clearly illustrates this is Europol, from which the UK's Rob Wainwright stepped down as Director earlier this year after 9 years in post. The UK made the largest contribution to Europol SOC (Serious and Organised Crime) Analysis Projects in 2016 and 2017:

12.5 per cent. The UK also makes the greatest contribution in terms of information in key areas: child sexual exploitation and abuse; firearms; money laundering; cyber; and modern slavery. After Germany, the UK makes the second-largest contribution to the Organised Immigration Crime Analysis Project.[9]

If the government is serious about focusing on the UK's future security relationship with the EU, rather than its internal splits, the first step should be to reconsider its self-imposed red lines. Michel Barnier has already highlighted these as a problem.[10] Yet in Barnier's position there is room for manoeuvre. While he says on the one hand that the UK "*cannot take part in the European Arrest Warrant*" he adds: "*This does not mean that we cannot work together on extradition*".[11]

To take just one of the red lines as an example: the Prime Minister has often heralded the end of the jurisdiction of the European Court of Justice (ECJ) in the UK. Yet, at the same time, having no role at all for the ECJ is totally unrealistic. Any free trade deal needs an arbitration mechanism. If the UK is to continue to participate in EU security infrastructure, then a role for the ECJ, alongside our own courts, needs to be considered. This could open up a whole new negotiation on the future security treaty. The Prime Minister has made a vague comment that "*when participating in EU agencies the UK will respect the remit of the European Court of Justice*"[12] but she needs to be more precise and go much further.

In conducting the negotiation, the government must emphasise the UK's contribution to EU security, and the mutually beneficial nature of European co-operation in dealing with the most serious organised crime on our continent. Citizens across Europe express support time and again when terrible terrorist atrocities occur, with social media enabling messages of condolence to be transmitted to thousands and thousands of people in an instant. Those links of solidarity should be given institutional expression by the UK government. It should reconsider its negotiating strategy as soon as possible.

---

1 According to the NCA, "European Arrest Warrant Statistics", available at www.nationalcrimeagency.gov.uk/publications/european-arrest-warrant-statistics

2 HM Government, "The Future Relationship Between the United Kingdom and European Union" (July 2018), available at https://assets.publishing.service.gov.uk/government/uploads/system/uploads/attachment_data/file/725288/The_future_relationship_between_the_United_Kingdom_and_the_European_Union.pdf, p.60.

3 Nick Hurd MP, "European Arrest Warrants: Written question – 147433" (4 June 2018), available at www.parliament.uk/business/publications/written-questions-answers-statements/written-question/Commons/2018-05-23/147433/

4 HM Government, "The Future Relationship Between the United Kingdom and European Union" (July 2018), available at https://assets.publishing.service.gov.uk/government/uploads/system/uploads/attachment_data/file/725288/The_future_relationship_between_the_United_Kingdom_and_the_European_Union.pdf, p.60.

5 The Prime Minister, "UK/EU Future Economic Partnership", *Hansard*, Volume 637, House of Commons (5 March 2018), available online at http://bit.ly/2OBi7uD

6 Michel Barnier, "Speech by Michel Barnier at the European Union Agency for Fundamental Rights", *European Commission: Press Release Database*, available at http://europa.eu/rapid/press-release_SPEECH-18-4213_en.htm

7 www.gov.uk/government/speeches/pm-speech-at-munich-security-conference-17-february-2018

8 European Union Committee, "Brexit: the proposed UK-EU security treaty" (11 July 2018), available at https://publications.parliament.uk/pa/ld201719/ldselect/ldeucom/164/16402.htm, paragraph 152.

9 EU Home Affairs Sub-Committee, Brexit: the proposed EU-UK security treaty: National Crime Agency, Supplementary Written Evidence: http://data.parliament.uk/writtenevidence/committeeevidence. svc/evidencedocument/eu-home-affairs-subcommittee/brexit-the-proposed-ukeu-security-treaty/written/86336.html

10 Michel Barnier, "Speech by Michel Barnier at the European Union Agency for Fundamental Rights", *European Commission: Press Release Database*, available at http://europa.eu/rapid/press-release_SPEECH-18-4213_en.htm: "Yet today we know that the UK is not ready to accept the free movement of people, the jurisdiction of the Court and the Charter of Fundamental Rights – for the Charter, this was confirmed last week by the House of Commons."

11 Michel Barnier, "Speech by Michel Barnier at the European Union Agency for Fundamental Rights", *European Commission: Press Release Database*, available at http://europa.eu/rapid/ press-release_SPEECH-18-4213_en.htm

12 www.gov.uk/government/speeches/pm-speech-at-munich-security-conference-17-february-2018

4 | EU PERSPECTIVE
FACING CHALLENGES TOGETHER
Nathalie Tocci and Paola Sartori

Both the EU and the UK have much to gain from a deep and comprehensive security and defence partnership after Brexit. To achieve this, both sides will need to be more flexible in the negotiations. Excessive rigidity on the EU's part risks a boomerang effect, forcing member states who want to cooperate with the UK to do so outside the EU framework.

Europe faces multiple and multifaceted challenges. External and internal security have become increasingly intertwined, while hybrid threats have blurred the civilian-military divide. Against this complex and fluid strategic landscape, close cooperation between the EU and the UK in a post Brexit world is crucial for the security of Europe and all its citizens.

The EU and the UK have remained on the same page when it comes to their assessment of the strategic defence and security landscape. The degree of analytical and prescriptive convergence between the EU Global Strategy for Foreign and Security Policy (EUGS) and the UK National Security Strategy and Strategic Defence Review is testimony to this fact. Issues that will remain front and centre of the EU and the UK's strategic approach include state fragility opening the way to terrorism and ungoverned spaces, the eruption and escalation of violent conflict to the east and south, Russia's assertiveness, an unpredictable America, and the growing strategic rivalry in east Asia. There are also the diffuse structural challenges stemming from climate change, connectivity, demography and the governance of the global commons. It is precisely the awareness of this fact that has made both the British government and the EU leadership determined to find common ground on security and defence in a post Brexit Europe.

Another positive is that the UK's decision to leave the Union has contributed to an unprecedented activism in European defence. Whereas the UK had been at the forefront of the push towards the Common Security and Defence Policy in the years following the Franco-British 1998 St Malò Declaration, after the Conservative Party's return to power in 2010, the UK government became sceptical of deeper European defence cooperation. The concern was that stepping up European defence would be to the detriment of the Atlantic Alliance. This has led some in Europe to see a silver lining in the UK's decision to leave: now that the British foot is off the brake of EU defence, the rest can get on with pursuing greater integration.

In addition to this, signalling European unity after the UK referendum result became an overarching political priority. Faced with deep intra-EU divisions over the Eurozone and migration, defence became the obvious function to demonstrate such unity of purpose. It is no wonder that it was high on the list of priorities, which emerged from the informal Bratislava summit of September 2017 held by the 27 on the future of the EU. The establishment of a Military Planning and Conduct Capability and the launch of the Coordinated Annual Review on Defence (CARD), the European Defence Fund (EDF), and the Permanent Structured Cooperation (PESCO) would probably not have happened had Britain decided to remain in the EU.

Yet the glass is only half full. In a post-Brexit Europe, the Union will lose one of its most militarily resourceful, expert and capable member states, significantly reducing the firepower of initiatives such as PESCO and the EDF. On its part, the UK will lose access to the force multiplier effects of European defence initiatives, and the UK will no longer be represented in the Council, the European External Action Service, the European Defence Agency and Europol, thus losing its influence on EU decision making.

It is precisely because of the mutual gains derived from ongoing cooperation and the severe mutual losses were such cooperation to decline, that the goal of a close and structured security and defence partnership between the EU and the UK is both desirable and attainable.

As far as PESCO is concerned, participating member states may invite third countries to join specific projects, provided conditions are met. These will be established by the Council by the end of 2018. As for the EDF, while the regulation for the European Defence Industrial Development Programme (EDIDP) was recently finalised, the regulation for the post-2010 EDF is under scrutiny by the Council and the parliament. Most notable is the fact that the Commission's proposal for the post 2020 EDF budget is more inclusive compared to the EDIDP, opening the fund also to European Free Trade Association (EFTA) members. In other words, a soft Brexit would enable the UK's participation in key instruments such as the EDF. By the same token, reaching an administrative arrangement with the European Defence Agency (EDA), along the lines of the one signed in December 2015 between the EDA and Ukraine, would allow ongoing cooperation with EDA activities both at the political-military level, as well as on technological and industrial aspects.

Brexit will also significantly affect the realm of internal security. The UK risks exiting the European Arrest

Warrant and losing access to EU databases, such as the European Criminal Record Information System (ECRIS). Without a proper arrangement, homeland data flows and police and judicial cooperation risk being suspended alto-gether to the severe detriment of both the UK and the EU. This would be particularly damaging in the fight against terrorism and organised crime. Reaching a comprehen-sive agreement is critical to the safety of both British and EU citizens.

The UK referendum was dominated by the narrative of a 'global Britain', juxtaposed to that of a European UK. The leave campaign argued for a fully 'sovereign' UK that would reinforce its standing internationally, by relying on its special relationship with the US, striking trade deals with rising powers such as China, and reinforcing its ties with the Commonwealth. Two years on, 'going global' seems a distant prospect for an internally and externally troubled Britain. A revised Anglo-American relationship is unlikely to compensate for the losses deriving from Brexit, especially given the US's increasing attention towards the Asia-Pacific. In addition, in China and the Commonwealth there is little appetite for a more independent Britain outside the EU. Any attempt to reinforce ties with Commonwealth countries could also clash with the anti-immigration agenda of the Brexiteers: a closer relationship with India for instance would likely require a relaxation of visa requirements, an anathema to those selling the illu-sion of "taking back control".

It is the growing appreciation of this reality that has probably led the UK to progressively soften its stance and assert its conviction to remain closely involved with the EU in the defence and security realm. The recently adopted UK white paper appears to pave the way towards a 'soft Brexit', with the UK closely aligned with the EU's single market, customs union and the European Court of Justice. Should such a scenario materialise, the EU and the UK will probably be able to define a deep and extensive security and defence partnership.[1]

Striking an arrangement that benefits both sides will require the EU to move beyond its 'red lines' and adopt a more flexible, forward looking and strategic perspective. In fact, while reasons behind the firm EU posture in the negotiations are understandably connected to broader considerations about the future of Europe, security and defence are peculiar briefs, which deserve the extra mile of flexibility and 'outside of the box' thinking. A more flexible approach should apply to the exchange of information as well as to the participation in capability development programmes. By contrast, excessive rigidity on the EU's side risks having a boomerang effect, as member states wishing to cooperate with the UK would likely find a way of doing so outside the EU framework.

Considering the variety of issues at stake, it is difficult to envisage a single comprehensive agreement covering all aspects of security and defence, let alone the broader Brexit deal. Therefore, moving towards a framework agreement to be updated and complemented with specific arrangements may be the wisest path to take. Such an approach would provide time to both parties to adjust and assess the appropriate scale and depth of the partnership. Both the EU and the UK have much to gain from a deep and comprehensive security and defence partnership. They have even more to lose from the absence thereof. A positive outcome is utterly within reach. Rationality, courage and creativity are the necessary ingredients for the EU and the UK to collectively contribute to the security of Europe, of its citizens and of the wider world.

---

1   For a scenario-based analysis on Brexit implications for the European Defence Industry, please refer to: Paola Sartori, Alessandro Marrone, Michele Nones, Looking Through the Fog of Brexit: Scenarios and

Implications for the European Defence Industry, in Documenti IAI 18|16, Rome, July 2018, www.iai.it/sites/default/files/iai1816.pdf

5 | EUROPEAN POPULAR NATIONALISM AND THE CRISIS OF SOCIAL DEMOCRACY

Wes Streeting

The economic crisis caused by a hard Brexit or the democratic deficit of a soft Brexit each risk fuelling Britain's populist right. The challenge facing the centre left today is whether we can bring our country back together around a politics that is patriotic, democratic and open to the world.

Nationalism is on the march again. Protectionism is back in vogue. Both were underlying factors in Britain's decision to leave the European Union. They helped to carry Donald Trump into the White House and marched brazenly through the streets of Charlottesville under the Nazi banner. They underpin the 'strong man' authoritarian governments in Putin's Russia, Erdogan's Turkey, Xi's China and even Abe's Japan.

The long tail of the global financial crisis, the economics of austerity, deindustrialisation and the hollowing out of towns and communities, have combined with concern about high levels of migration to form a perfect storm that has battered centre right parties and shipwrecked the centre left.

The success of European popular nationalism

Emmanuel Macron may have entered the Elyseé Palace following a decisive win over Marine Le Pen, but his victory was the precursor to a wave of success for far right parties across the continent. In September 2017, Angela Merkel had to face the grim reality of the first major far right presence in the German Bundestag since the Second World War; the Alternative for Germany (AfD) won 94 seats with the support of one in eight voters. The following month, Andrej Babis led his anti-immigrant ANO Party to victory in the Czech Republic and the far-right Freedom Party entered the Austrian Government as part of a governing coalition after winning one in four votes. In March 2018, the anti-establishment Five Star Movement became Italy's largest party, while The League, a vehemently anti-immigrant party leapt from four per cent to 18 per cent of the popular vote, replacing Silvio Berlusconi's Forza Italia as the dominant party on the right of Italian politics. From Golden Dawn in Greece on seven per cent to the Swiss People's Party on 29 per cent, the most recent national election results across Europe show alarming levels of support for right wing populist parties from Scandanavia to Southern Europe.

Right wing populists have not enjoyed the same electoral success at the ballot box in the UK, but something more sinister lurks beneath the surface of the body politic. Hope Not Hate warns that Britain is facing a 'growing and changing far right threat'. Although the British National Party has collapsed and organisational membership of far right groups is at its lowest point in twenty-five years, their online presence is increasing and far right terrorism and violent extremism is on the rise.

The right wing populist moment in British politics was successful in the EU referendum. For eurosceptics on the left, the European Union is an antidemocratic project that sees too much power exercised by unaccountable elites and a capitalist project that undermines the ability of nation states to take decisions that benefit the people. For eurosceptics on the right, it is not simply that they believe that decisions would be better exercised at a national level; they reject a rules-based global economy. Theirs is a libertarian vision of deregulation, unfettered free markets and the UK as an offshore tax haven. For Donald Trump, Brexit suits his protectionist agenda as he rips up free trade agreements and paralyses the World Trade Organisation. Anti-capitalists and 'Wild West' capitalists arrive at the same conclusion with very different motivations.

Social democracy missing in action

The rise of populism and European popular nationalism is a symptom of a deeper crisis at the heart of neo-liberalism caused by its failure to deliver for economy and society. Liberal democracy is under threat as enlightenment values like reason, science and religious tolerance are crushed by the rampaging forces of a post-truth movement.

Amidst the maelstrom, social democracy has been missing in action. Centre left governments paid a heavy price for being at the wheel when the car crashed in 2007–8 during the global financial crisis, but if it were simply a case of 'wrong place, wrong time', social democrats could have recovered by now. Third way politics, so electorally successful for a while that people talked excitedly about a 'progressive century', was too indifferent to the worst excesses of globalisation and the reckless, destructive greed of financial capital. The tax receipts were coming in, the economy was booming and centre left governments, like New Labour under Tony Blair, were happily ploughing record investment into public services to reverse years of decay and decline. In the aftermath of the crash, the centre left tradition that prided itself on being able to modernise struggled to modernise, presenting itself as a technocratic, managerial project based on offering incremental change when the moment demanded something economically transformational.

The Brexit fallacy and the progressives' Brexit dilemma

We see the same lack of ambition playing out in the Labour Party's response to Brexit. Labour's old centre left establishment, now reeling from defeat inside the party, are behaving as if the future is a binary choice between the voters of Streatham and the voters of Stoke-on-Trent: between liberal metropolitan voters in our big cities and our traditional working class base in the old industrial heartlands. Labour's new establishment under Jeremy Corbyn is struggling to hold this fragile electoral coalition together – the Corbyn project itself a coalition that embraces old-school eurosceptic leftists and idealistic young pro-Europeans.

The Brexit that people voted for cannot be delivered. A hard Brexit would address voters' concerns about sovereignty and migration, but with significant economic harm. A soft Brexit would reduce the economic risk, but at the expense of democracy and sovereignty because the UK would be subjected to rules over which it has no formal say. Both scenarios – economic crisis and democratic deficit – represent a manifesto of misery and despair for increasingly weary voters who already believe that their political leaders don't keep their promises and lack real answers to address their hopes and fears. Both risk a populist backlash and create fertile breeding ground for Britain's nascent far right. This is the heart of the progressives' Brexit dilemma.

Contesting the nature of modern nationhood

Writing for the *Guardian* in 2011, Dagenham and Rainham MP Jon Cruddas and leading Blue Labour thinker Jonathan

Rutherford urged the Labour Party to 'seize the politics of identity and belonging from the right', arguing that 'Labour has prospered when it has contested the nature of modern nationhood' and 'must do so again because a sense of foreboding is taking hold in our country and the right seeks to alter its essential character'. Their warning was prescient.

What we haven't yet figured out is how we can marry 'patriotism and place' with globalisation. Protecting what matters to people – family, friendship, community, work, national identity and a sense of belonging – requires a more substantial political patriotism than simply faith, family and flag. Without an open and outward looking nation state, engaged with the world and acting with others, the flag will be battered by global headwinds, the family will be unemployed and their prayers will go unanswered.

The challenges confronting Britain and the world today require a complete re-imagination of global governance built around the local state, the national state and the global state.

We have a global economic system that is decentralised and increasingly digitised – paying less regard to borders and places. It is defining where people work, where they live and how much they're paid. We've already seen what happens when nation states fail to govern effectively: the wholesale loss of jobs, boarded-up town centres and ordinary people paying the price for the worst excesses of the 'masters of the universe' in global financial services. The next phase of globalisation will continue apace, with the centre of economic gravity shifting to the East and the rise of new tech oligarchs, who already believe themselves to be more powerful, more relevant and more righteous than national governments.

Big questions arise about how we ensure that citizens' rights, protections and voices are protected and promoted not diminished. This isn't a conversation to surrender to libertarians and authoritarians. In 1945, the Labour Government played a leading role in creating international institutions to prevent another world war. Today we need to lead the world again in a conversation about how we create new global institutions and frameworks to create inclusive growth, curtail the excesses of global capital and rebuild international relations around a rules-based system fit for the modern world.

Labour is currently in the foothills of the debate about how we bring about our national renewal. There is widespread consensus across the party about the need for investment in our public services and national infrastructure. Labour's 'Build it in Britain' campaign is speaking to a well understood common sense that measuring value in procurement isn't simply about the lowest price, but wider value in terms of jobs, communities and sovereign capability. The public believe we're better placed than the Tories to protect the NHS, tackle the housing crisis and educate our children. But they are yet to be convinced that we can be trusted to defend Queen and country, provide law and order and spend their money wisely. There is a proud and patriotic tradition on the centre left of supporting our armed forces; being tough on crime as well as its causes; that expects people to pay their fair share of taxes as the price for a civilised society and that spends money wisely. The British people want our country to be open to global talent and open hearted to refugees, but they want to know that everyone is abiding by a set of rules that are firm and fair.

Finally, we need to deliver the greatest redistribution of power and resources from central to local government in British history. On housing, education and skills, health and social care, transport and economic development, local government is better placed to make decisions in the interests of local communities. It offers app-addicted citizens with expectations of personalised services a greater possibility to be involved in the design and delivery of their public services, replacing the marketisation dogma of competition over collaboration and citizens as customers with a new public service ethos of co-operation with citizens as co-producers.

The twentieth century is fighting the twenty-first. Every great Labour government has been elected with a compelling national story about the condition of Britain and how they intended to change it to meet the challenges of the day in the interests of the common good. The economic crisis caused by a hard Brexit or the democratic deficit of a soft Brexit both risk fuelling Britain's populist right. The challenge facing the centre left today is whether we can bring our country back together around a politics that is patriotic, democratic and open to the world.

6 | EU PERSPECTIVE
THE SEARCH FOR
A PROGRESSIVE PATRIOTISM

Maria Maltschnig

The Austrian example shows that progressive patriotism is not about defining ourselves against others, or closing ourselves off from the world. Instead, we must build a patriotism that is based on the fact that wealth and social progress have been built by the many and not by the few.

Brexit is just one example of a rising cultural divide across the western world. We just have to look at the election of Donald Trump and the rising support for right wing populism in many European countries. A growing number of people are prioritising their national identity and putting immigration at the top of their list of political concerns. On the other hand, there are also a growing number of educated urban professionals that actively value living in a globalised world. The challenge for the left is to bridge this divide, and part of that must be developing a progressive sense of national identity.

Obviously, for a vast majority of EU citizens, their national identity is much stronger than their European identity. This is neither surprising nor the most pressing challenge the European Union faces. There are national languages, children are taught their nation's history in school. National broadcasting companies and national newspapers still dominate our media consumption and most people only travel abroad occasionally. This is not a threat to European integration per se. One can identify as Austrian, Italian, Polish, etc. and be a confident European citizen at the same time. Neither Brexit nor the election gains of right-wing parties have their roots in the mere existence of national identities.

So where did it go wrong? How has national identity become identified with right wing political agendas and how has it become such a powerful election issue? One theory links this development to the fundamental change in working life: the individualisation of career paths and the decline of collective identities, especially in working class environments, has left a gap that people try to fill by searching for other identities.

This is not an issue for those who benefit from individualisation and who have the freedom to work and travel wherever it suits them. Those people are young, highly educated, and many of them live in cities. They are part of a "global class" and appreciate multiculturalism and the possibilities they gain from living in the European Union. For people who did not benefit from the changes of the last decades, things are harder. These people are older, without higher education, and many of them live in rural areas and towns. We have to overcome this cultural divide and restore and strengthen the social balance in industrialised economies.

Two years ago, a progressive patriotism was an important part of the election campaign of the winner of the presidential elections in Austria. After the candidates of the traditional leading parties – the conservatives and the social democrats – failed to make it to the run-off, the two final candidates were Norbert Hofer from the far right Freedom Party and Alexander Van der Bellen from the Green Party. The socio-demographic divide of the supporters of the two candidates was very similar to those of the leave and remain campaigns in the Brexit referendum.

The right wing candidate's campaign was based on a populist, flag-waving blunt nationalism, whereas the green candidate relied on an optimistic patriotic approach, accompanied by courage, confidence and solidarity. Pictures showed Alexander Van der Bellen in the surroundings of the Tyrolian Alps with the slogan "Home needs Solidarity". Widely popular traditional Austrian singers and songwriters and even several former leaders of the conservative party publicly supported Van der Bellen. All of this successfully targeted the political centre.

In the end the result was a clear victory (54 per cent) for Van der Bellen. His progressive patriotism might not have been the leading election motive among his voters, but it helped to ease a potential polarisation on the matter of national identity.

However, one year later at the parliamentary elections, an even larger majority (58 per cent) voted for the two right wing parties. Though the social democrats gained the highest number of former Van der Bellen voters (990,000), 700,000 voters moved to the conservatives. The so called "Van der Bellen coalition" included a large number of moderate conservatives who opposed a right wing populist president. Establishing a progressive nationalism is neither the only, nor the most promising, strategy to give those who are searching for an alternative to their lost collective identity a new one. It is also not the first thing social democrats think about. We fight for good jobs and functioning communities. We encourage people to engage in trade unions and civil society projects. We demand democratic structures not only in politics but also in schools, universities and the workplace. All these elements can provide identity and confidence. But we should also get better at talking about patriotism.

The Austrian Social Democratic Party will decide on its new manifesto at the party's convention in October 2018. The manifesto was drafted with the help of several thousand party members – as well as academics and civil society representatives – who contributed their ideas both on an online platform and at more than a hundred debates that took place all over Austria earlier this year. Among the questions the party members debated were questions on what defines us as a nation and why we are proud of our country. The debate resulted in the following paragraph in the draft manifesto:

"Our patriotism does not focus against others. It aims to advance our country. Those who love their country, help to improve it. We are confident Austrians because Austria is a country with a strong welfare state and a high level of social commitment. Austria is a country of social balance, solidarity and social cohesion. It is a country in which economic progress is linked to prosperity for everyone. We are proud of our country's achievements because they are the result of the hard work of many dedicated men and women."

A progressive patriotism is not about defining ourselves against others, or closing ourselves off from the world. Instead, we must build a patriotism that is based on the fact that wealth and social progress has been built by the many and not by the few.

7 | A NEW POLITICAL ECONOMY BASED ON EVERYDAY LIVES

Rachel Reeves

The Brexit vote represented a popular rejection of our current economic model, which has disempowered ordinary people and widened inequality. We must construct a new left political economy which focuses on people's everyday lives, and gets to grips with the concerns that dominated the referendum campaign.

It is now more than two years since the UK voted to leave the European Union. In that time, Westminster politics has been in constant tumult. We have seen leadership elections in both major parties, the rise of Theresa May who promised to address the deep economic and social problems which led to Brexit, and then the extraordinary 2017 general election campaign and its outcome. Meanwhile, the government's handling of negotiations has been catastrophic and so many of the leave campaign's promises have already proven false. For all of this, the problems which triggered Brexit remain almost exactly as they were in June 2016.

Brexit exposed and exacerbated our country's divisions, particularly along lines of geography, education, age and class.[1] For Labour these divides were particularly stark: while the remain campaign enjoyed a comfortable majority in London, leave had a twelve-point lead in our heartlands beyond the capital.[2] While the 2017 general election saw

Labour make gains in seats like Kensington and Canterbury, we also suffered setbacks in areas like the Midlands and the North-East which had voted strongly to leave the EU. If Labour is to form the next government, it must understand the factors that motivated leave voters in those areas and offer a political prospectus that speaks to them.

Our failed economic model

That starts by understanding that the Brexit vote represented a popular rejection of our current economic model, which has disempowered ordinary people and widened inequality. Over the last three or four decades, our economy has increasingly become based on wealth extraction rather than wealth creation.

The historian David Edgerton recently argued that the 'great transformation' of Britain's economy under Margaret Thatcher, combined with Britain's reintegration into an increasingly globalised economy, had such a profound effect that 'it no longer made sense to talk of a national economy... the United Kingdom ceased to have a distinctly national capitalism and became instead a major financial centre, now largely for the capital of others.'[3] Government has been too indifferent to the economic and cultural consequences of this shift, especially for working-class voters across the country, who became increasingly disconnected from mainstream politics and the Labour party in particular.[4] While many people in our cities and university towns benefited enormously from these changes and the new opportunities they presented, for many other people, the experience was primarily one of loss. Leaving the European Union does not represent a solution to these problems, but for many people the Brexit referendum became an opportunity to send a message.

Britain's entry into the EEC in 1973 was a product, not a cause, of the country's relative economic decline. In practice, membership helped to arrest that decline in the following four decades. However, membership has coincided with the collapse of the post-war social-democratic settlement and the decline of British global power. Since then, the balance of power between capital and labour has shifted decisively away from working people. Businesses and markets have become detached from communities and countries. Entire industries have disappeared and left in their wake a legacy of unemployment, ill-health and community breakdown. Precarious and exploitative forms of work have continued to proliferate, often facilitated by migrant labour. Short-term shareholder returns have come to prevail over all other considerations. Privatisation and outsourcing have allowed the emergence of a crony capitalism which – temporarily – allowed companies like Carillion to thrive as corporate partners to the state. For many, EU membership seemed emblematic of these wider changes. The right's willingness, over decades, to capitalise on this and reinforce a sense that it was the EU – and not the decisions of domestic politicians – which was in large part to blame was a key contributing factor in the leave vote.

The frailties of the post-Thatcher settlement were devastatingly exposed by the 2008 financial crisis and its aftermath. What GDP growth there has been over the last decade has not been felt in real incomes. Andy Haldane, Chief Economist of the Bank of England, has charted how any post-2008 recovery has been restricted almost exclusively to London and the South East of England, those who are already asset-rich, home-owners, and those over fifty.[5] We have ended up with an economy that rewards those who already have wealth while making it ever harder for those who do not to obtain any. As the Oxford economist Ben Ansell has shown, who has won and who has lost from this situation maps closely onto the Brexit vote: house prices closely correlate to the Brexit vote

41

between regions, constituencies, wards and even house-holds. The lower the house prices in an area, the more likely its residents were to vote to Leave.[6] Meanwhile, the forty-year experience of globalisation, neoliberalism and the rapid growth of new technologies has deprived people of power over their circumstances, and often a sense of belonging and identity. Faced with these changes, the central state has been too slow and too cautious in devolving to communities the real power they need to compensate for these losses.

A new focus on the everyday economy

Nothing less than a new and ambitious left-wing political economy can address these problems. This must equip us with the tools to address the fundamental weaknesses of the British economy, and also speak to those things which matter most to people: good work; strong families, and happy, healthy places to live.

A new approach needs to begin with the everyday economy – those sectors like care and retail which are characterised by high employment, but also too often low wages and low productivity. Yet, we depend on them for happy, healthy lives and communities. Crucially, these sectors are found in every part of the country, they disproportionately employ people in low-paid and precarious work, and they have considerable scope for improvements in productivity and working conditions.

So, what might such an agenda look like?[7] Labour local authorities across the country are already showing what can be done to build power by working alongside, and supporting, civil society. Labour needs a plan for how central government can support and encourage work like this.

A unit for local wealth building, based in number 10, could be tasked with building local capacity, and organising the cross-departmental collaboration necessary for its implementation. We need to spread capital across the country with a British investment bank, the partly-nationalised Royal Bank of Scotland or a decentralised Citizens' Wealth Fund providing commercial loans on a long-term basis. 'Anchor institutions' such as hospitals, universities, large businesses and schools can be used to help develop local economies through their procurement policy, by driving up wages through Living Wage deals, and by spreading innovation through the supply chains of often poorly performing companies.

We need reforms to improve the quality of work, to boost wages and raise the profile of the worker voice in all sectors of the everyday economy. That means prioritising productivity, and the integration of technology in a way which improves rather than displaces jobs, in these sectors as part of Britain's industrial strategy.[8] Workers' representation on boards and improved collective bargaining rights will be key to giving employees more power in the workplace. And Labour should champion the creation of new royal colleges for sectors like social care, to raise the esteem of these professions, advise on policy change, and ensure it is the people who know best that are setting standards for professional practice and training.

A radical new economic agenda, however, would count for little if the government leads us to a "no deal" Brexit. In fact, the structural factors that caused the vote would most likely be worsened in such a situation, potentially sending the economy into a nose dive: no one voted leave to be poorer or for jobs to be lost. Those who voted for Brexit were misled by the false promises from the leave campaign such as the bogus claim about £350 million extra a week for the NHS if we left the EU.

I firmly believe that membership of the customs union and the single market is the best way of protecting jobs and growth and providing a stable platform from which

Labour can build its new economic settlement. Staying in the customs union and the single market is the best outcome for our economy and the best outcome for households across Britain.

But we also need to look at why people voted for Brexit. We cannot continue to neglect the underlying problems behind the leave vote. That would be a catastrophic failure of all those involved in politics. That means constructing a new left political economy able to speak to people's everyday experiences, and getting to grips with the concerns which dominated the referendum campaign, including free movement of labour. Twice in the last century, in the years following 1945 and 1979, Britain's economic model and social settlement was radically reshaped. The convulsions that have shaken domestic and global politics since 2015 are a warning of the consequence if Labour cannot do so again.

---

1   See, Yougov: How Britain Voted, https://yougov.co.uk/news/ 2016/06/27/how-britain-voted/

2   www.theguardian.com/politics/2016/jun/25/left-behind-eu-referendum-vote-ukip-revolt-brexit

3   David Edgerton, *The Rise and Fall of the British Nation*, (London: Allen Lane, 2018), p.xxiii.

4   Geoffrey Evans and James Tilley, *The New Politics of Class*, (Oxford: Oxford University Press, 2017); see also, Rachel Reeves, 'Labour's Class Coalitions, Then and Now: A Response to The New Politics of Class by Geoff Evans and James Tilley', *Political Quarterly*, (Vol.88, No.4, October–December 2017), pp.702–6.

5   Andy Haldane, 'Whose Recovery?', speech given in Port Talbot, Wales, 30th June 2016. See here: www.bankofengland.co.uk/-/media/boe/files/speech/2016/whose-recovery.pdf?la=en&hash= 11C0C02AF21765A92854B0CA670EE85E8F900B96

6   Ben Ansell, 'Housing, Credit and Brexit', paper presented at the University of Wisconsin, April 2017. Available here: http://users.ox.ac.uk/~polf0487/papers/Ansell%20Brexit%20Memo.pdf

7   For more, see: Rachel Reeves, *The Everyday Economy*, (2018). Available here www.scribd.com/document/374425087/Rachel-Reeves-The-Everyday-Economy

8   For some excellent ideas, see: Cameron Tait, *At the Crossroads: The Future of British Retail*, (London: Fabian Society, 2017).

8 | EU PERSPECTIVE
BOOSTING INVESTMENT
Stephany Griffiths Jones

Both the EU and the UK need to increase public and private investment in their economies. Labour's plan for a national investment bank is a welcome step, but this must work alongside the European Investment Bank which has financed many key projects in the UK.

It would be best for the economies of both the EU and UK if Brexit did not happen. But if it does, it makes sense to maintain close links. From a progressive perspective, the UK and the EU should have shared priorities. These must include good, well paid jobs and the development of an environmentally sustainable model of growth. To achieve these aims both the EU and UK must increase both public and private investment in their economies.

The level of total investment to GDP across the EU is fairly low, only 20.1 per cent in 2017. This is significantly lower than ten years before when it reached 22.4 per cent. Amongst EU member states, the 2017 level of investment to GDP was lowest in Greece (12.6 per cent) and Portugal (16.2 per cent). These two countries were severely hit by the crisis, and have faced creditor imposed austerity. But third lowest was the UK with only 16.9 per cent, a consequence of self-imposed austerity measures.

A good way to increase EU public investment would be through what German economist Peter Bofinger has called the 'lighthouse initiative'. Named to signify the brighter future that Europeans deserve, the initiative would allow Eurozone governments to increase public investment by up to 1 per cent of each country's GDP above the Maastricht limit, provided the investment clearly enhanced growth. If all Eurozone countries implemented the initiative, we could see an increase in public investment of approximately €500 billion over the next five years. That is 1 per cent of the Eurozone GDP.

When there are scarce resources available, and insufficient demand, as is the case in many EU economies, there is a strong case that public investment encourages private investment, as leading economists like Joseph Stiglitz have shown. Furthermore, the International Monetary Fund has strongly argued that the German, Dutch or other credit-worthy governments can, at present, borrow funds so cheaply that these resources, if well invested, will have yields well above the cost of borrowing. As a result future debt to GDP levels would fall rather than rise, as growth would increase.

The lighthouse initiative to boost public investment would be a complement to the already existing Juncker plan, also known as the European Fund for Strategic Investment (EFSI). This helps finance private investment in strategic sectors, like the green and digital economies, as well as helping to fund small and medium enterprises. EFSI is projected to stimulate up to approximately €500 billion additional private investment, in the 2015–2020 period.

It is important to point out that EFSI works particularly well as it co-finances both with the private and the public financial sector. It has been doing more of this recently with the latter, including with national public development banks like Germany's KfW. This has helped catalyse investment in new sectors such as renewable energy, and in funding small and medium enterprises, especially when private banks have been reluctant to do so.

The UK Labour party's plan to create a public development bank – called the National Investment Bank – is a very welcome step. There are lots of successful countries such as Germany, Japan and South Korea who use a similar approach, and they provide an important instrument for economic transformation. A national investment bank will be especially important in the UK where the investment rate is extremely low.

It will also be important for the new UK national investment bank to work with the European Investment Bank (EIB), which has expanded significantly in recent years. The EIB has expertise in lending for key infrastructure projects, and support for SMEs, including through venture capital. It has in the UK recently co-financed Crossrail, new social housing, school and university buildings, as well as provided key finance for renewable energy projects.

In a recent interview with the *Financial Times*, the president of the EIB said he would like the UK to remain a full member, and implied that this would be a win-win situation both for the UK and the EIB. This would be beneficial for the EIB as it would keep the capital of one of its largest shareholders intact so it can maintain its current lending capacity. It would also clearly benefit the UK, as it would avoid a major gap in long term funding provided by the EIB for key activities. It would also allow a future Labour government to have an ideal partner for the national investment bank.

9 | EU PERSPECTIVE
STRENGTHENING THE SOCIAL PILLAR
Tomáš Petříček

There has been insufficient focus on the social causes of Brexit, and the EU must address this. Brexit provides an opportunity and an impetus for better cooperation in social policy, because the UK has tended to be reluctant to support greater integration in this area.

The debate about Brexit has largely emphasised the economic impact on the UK and on the Union. It risks jobs and growth in the UK and causes problems for EU member states. The political impact of Brexit has also been widely discussed. The position of the EU in the world will be weakened without the UK. But one area that has not been sufficiently considered is the social impact.

The UK's decision to leave the EU was driven by social problems, especially rising inequality and uneven distribution of investment. These problems are common across Europe. There is rising inequality, the benefits of economic growth are not trickling down to large portions of the population, and there is growing anxiety about an unpredictable future. Stronger social cohesion and faster social convergence will be two issues that will need to be pushed up the political agenda of the European Union if we are to address people's concerns and regain their support for the European project.

To some extent, Brexit provides an opportunity to develop and implement a stronger social dimension to the EU. Britain has been traditionally reluctant to support the social pillar of European integration. It rejected the concept of a 'social Europe' in 1980s. It opposed the social chapter which was attached to the Maastricht treaty.

Brexit may therefore facilitate better cooperation in social policy for the remaining 27 countries. There have already been some moves which support this theory. For example, the EU launched the new European pillar of social rights. This was followed by the social summit for fair jobs and growth which took place last November in Gothenburg. The European Commission would like to revive the European social dialogue.

Brexit also presents a strong impetus to address the causes that makes existing social strategies relatively ineffective. At the core of the debate has to be the European employment strategy. If we are to strengthen social cohesion, we need to shift from a quantitative employment strategy to a qualitative one. Social democracy has promoted the concept of good jobs for more than ten years now. It is time that this becomes the central concept of the European social strategy. This will inevitably require new labour market regulations at the European level which will strike a new balance between job flexibility and worker protection. Establishing European collective bargaining, for example, might be easier with the absence of the UK. This could contribute to closing pay gaps between workers from different member states.

The Union will also need to find effective tools to close the economic and social gaps among the member states. There has been a substantial and enduring income gap between the Euro area and non-Euro area. This gap has not narrowed since 2004, even though income has increased in both areas. The European Union has not been able to tackle this problem, causing concern in some member states. It also makes it harder to find compromise on some elements of European social policy, such as minimum salary standards.

Another area where a stronger regulatory framework will be needed relates to public services. Access to health care, social services or education is key for strengthening social cohesion in Europe.

Brexit is unfortunate and it has considerable economic and political costs. But it also presents an opportunity for the European Union to strengthen its social pillar and to put social cohesion and social convergence at the centre of policy making.

10 | OUR BEST HOPE IS EACH OTHER

Lisa Nandy

For too long we have accepted that immigration and community are at odds. But there is a sensible, decent majority in this country who believe in a global, tolerant, open, outward facing, and diverse Britain. We must hand people the knowledge and power to control their own lives.

Immigration has long been a contentious issue on the left. This is reflected in the instruction issued by Labour to its activists in the 2015 election to "move the conversation on" when it arose on the doorstep.[1]

With the UK facing immediate and hard choices in the coming months, the need for a clear stance is undeniable. But more than two years since a referendum that sent shock waves through Westminster, we still have far too little understanding of what got us here, and consequently, too little idea of how to respond.

The dominant narrative that has found a home on the left is that leave voters were racist 'little Englanders', or insufficiently engaged in politics to understand the consequences of their choice. This completely fails to understand the complexity and strength of feeling across the country.

The majority of those who voted leave have consistently refused to vote for openly racist parties, like the BNP. These parties are still viewed as toxic by most people. For generations, in the words of playwright David Edgar, "*millions of working class people have fought racism and fight it still because it's the right thing to do"*. Towns like mine, in Wigan, who overwhelmingly voted to leave the EU have a long history of internationalism. Across Lancashire, textile workers stood shoulder to shoulder with Indian cotton pickers at great personal cost when they went out on strike several decades ago, and those values and principles are still palpable today.

There is little sense in leave voting towns and villages that UKIP speaks for them. Across the board, UKIP support has collapsed since 2015. To accept that this roar of noise was an endorsement of UKIP values obscures our understanding of why people voted to leave and clouds our ability to develop a sustainable response.

While the 'little Englander' narrative has gone unchallenged, Rob Ford of Manchester University points out that attitudes to immigration have become much more positive, strikingly across both the leave and remain, socially liberal and socially conservative divides.[2] This has gone largely unnoticed by advocates for a liberal, humane immigration policy.

The explanation for this complicated picture relates to globalisation and the way our economy has developed. A significant section of the population, who live outside of the urban centres, haven't benefitted from global opportunities. In those same areas we have also witnessed the loss of the things that tie communities together. Good jobs, community assets, and thriving high streets are the beating heart of a community. The EU came to embody a sense of frustration with the effects of globalisation, while the referendum provided an outlet for it.

Over time we have fractured into two groups: those who are globally connected and those who aren't. This global divide, between those who have opportunity and those who do not, was a running theme through the referendum campaign. Graduates have very different views about immigration to people who didn't go on to university.

People disconnected from the global economy look at the EU and see a system that favours the skilled and mobile at their expense. The EU has undoubtedly brought benefits to the country as a whole, but it has allowed successive governments to fill gaps in the labour market without having to invest in young people in towns like mine.

Across France, Germany, and the UK, there are young people who aren't grateful that we can attract migrants to work in healthcare or in industry, because they have lost training grants and nursing bursaries and no longer have the opportunity to get those jobs themselves. The remain campaign messages fell flat in communities where life experiences and priorities are a million miles away from those who penned them. What use is warning of economic catastrophe to people who are already struggling to get by? These communities have watched us defend a system that gives advantage to the skilled and mobile at the expense of them and their families. Now they have learnt, as Bevan once said, that 'silent pain evokes no response'.[3]

They are ordinary people in decent neighbourhoods with a home and a mortgage, a job and a family. But life has become harder over recent decades as jobs and opportunities have moved to the cities, depriving people of the chance to live near their children and grandchildren. Jobs have also become increasingly insecure and wages haven't kept up with prices, making the mortgage payment more of a struggle. The loss of disposable income has pushed high streets into decline and cost us community institutions. The result is fractured families and communities and an erosion of any sense of hope about the future.

This drives a deep sense of loss and a sense that the country that has staked out its future on a set of values that are at odds to their own. While some expressed anger in the referendum, for many the prospect of change had briefly brought hope flickering back to life.

While people might accept, or even, as Rob Ford has highlighted, feel increasing positivity towards immigration, they do not accept the rules of the game being written for them by people who live very different lives and have a totally different experience of playing it.

It is no longer sustainable for decisions to be made hundreds or thousands of miles away, changing lives and communities without the ability to challenge decisions and hold people to account.

We also need more honesty, integrity and clarity than in the past. On immigration Labour is often, as Tawney put it, "*hesitant in action because divided in mind*". We owe it to the public to be clear. Immigration matters to our lives and our economy. In areas like agriculture and social care it is critical to protect it. The most straightforward way to achieve this after Brexit is through continued access to the single market and we should be clear that this is preferable to tighter controls on immigration, if that is the choice. The evidence suggests that now would be a good time to find a hearing.

This should go hand in hand with opportunities for young people. If 'for the many not the few' is to have meaning we must reject a system that pits immigrants and citizens against one another, forcing us to pick a side. A commitment to investing in people, from early years all the way through to a renewed commitment to lifelong learning, has been and must become again a fundamental, non-negotiable part of a socialist vision.

There are 3.5 million EU citizens in the UK who deserve clarity about their position after 2020 and Labour should guarantee their rights to live and work in the UK. The opportunity to advance science, culture and study across Europe has brought huge benefits to us, our universities, our healthcare and our lives and we should continue to participate in shared programmes like Erasmus, paying our contributions and pulling our weight.

But a commitment to providing people with much more control over their own lives must extend to every community in the UK. It means a radical approach. Decisions about immigration are among many areas, like housing, planning, licensing, arts, culture and transport, where we deny communities the ability to make decisions for fear they'll get it wrong. But in doing so we have denied people the opportunity to shape their own communities and take control over their lives.

This is not consistent with our traditions. As Attlee said, socialists: *"do not think of human beings as a herd to be fed and watered and kept in security. They think of them as individuals co-operating together to make a fine collective life. For this reason socialism is a more exacting creed than that of its competitors. It does not demand submission and acquiescence, but active and constant participation in common activities".*

Immigration is one area where devolving the right to make decisions about the placement of refugees, skills funding and the use of migration impact funds, would create a more sustainable, and I suspect humane, outcome. I've seen it in my own constituency when a decision by Serco to place, overnight, a hundred young refugee men into a hotel in a small village in my constituency caused chaos until people were empowered with knowledge and the ability to act. The warm response – sparking food and clothing donations, the opening up of homes and community institutions and the rejection of the far right – was overwhelming.

For too long we have accepted that immigration and community are at odds. But there is a sensible, decent committed majority in this country who believe in a global, tolerant, open, outward facing, and diverse Britain and the future must belong to them. Progress is not inevitable but by handing people the knowledge and power to control their own lives, it can thrive. This requires us to have the courage of our convictions that has been lacking for too long. But the public should be our source of confidence. For all the division in Britain, our best hope remains each other.

---

1 www.telegraph.co.uk/news/politics/labour/11293433/Revealed-Labour-MPs-told-not-to-campaign-on-immigration-in-secret-Ukip-strategy-document.html

2 https://medium.com/@robfordmancs/how-have-attitudes-to-immigration-changed-since-brexit-e37881f55530#.83b877l3d

3 Bevan, In Place of Fear, 1952.

11 | EU PERSPECTIVE
IMMIGRATION MANAGEMENT
DOESN'T END AT THE BORDER
Sandro Gozi

Immigration is a crucial issue across the European Union. The EU must act as a single entity in response and recognise that immigration management doesn't end at the border.

Immigration is one of the crucial issues of our time. All recent elections, at every level and in every country, had immigration at the centre of the campaign. Immigration was also a key driver of the Brexit result, much more important than the empty promises about the NHS, or the traditional British antipathy towards European bureaucracy.

The leave campaign, organised around their slogan of 'take back control', built an argument around regaining control of borders. I agree with the idea of taking back border control. What divides me from leave campaigners, and from many of the European nationalists, is that I want to manage European borders rather than the borders of individual member states.

It would be ridiculous to try and manage the huge challenge of migration by adopting 27 (or 28) different policies. This is, and will be in the future, the most challenging issue to deal with for the European Union. If the EU does not act as a single entity on this issue, it will not be able to demonstrate that it can manage the whole phenomenon, and will end up once again in the eye of the storm of nationalist attacks.

A number of mistakes have clearly been made to get us to this point. Those who governed the single member states, as well as the European elites, underestimated the impact of immigration on our societies and communities. This has led to a huge range of different answers from member states, which do not constitute a coherent policy towards the issue. Some countries, such as Hungary, thought only about building border walls. Others had to focus on the problem in the Mediterranean Sea (Italy, Greece and Spain). Others focused on domestic problems. The UK case is peculiar because for many years it witnessed high flows of migration from within the European Union. Tens of thousands of skilled and unskilled Italians leave Italy looking for a job in the UK every year.

Immigration management does not end at the border. We must consider how governments can ensure integration and protection for the integrity of local communities. We must also ensure acceptable living conditions for migrants.

When focusing on non-EU migrants, arguably a more crucial concern for leave voters than EU migrants, the UK should look to successful approaches on the continent. Italy is undoubtedly one of the best examples, and I'm not just saying that because I'm Italian. The Sistema Protezione Richiedenti Asilo e Rifugiati (SPRAR) is based on a network of local authorities, and sustained with a national fund. A capillary reception system was chosen, so as to avoid enormous camps and to guarantee measures of information, assistance and orientation to help ensure socio-economic integration. The third sector is actively involved in the SPRAR system, with the aim of engaging public and private actors in the integration process and encouraging local communities to participate in the integration process.

Italy is also at the forefront of another crucial issue: the management of unaccompanied minors. Italian law states that unaccompanied foreign minors cannot be expelled from Italian territory, and provides them with a specific and distinct reception system. Protecting the best interests of children is at the heart of the policy and every effort is taken to ensure a good home and education are provided.

Another example of best practice is the Swedish one. No other EU country has historically received as many asylum seekers per inhabitant as Sweden, and Sweden undoubtedly has one of the best reception systems in Europe. The starting point is the Swedish Migration Board: migrants applying for asylum are granted not only shared accommodation, but also a personal account and a credit card to cover expenses for food, clothing, personal hygiene or any other personal need. All these measures are designed to help refugees and asylum seekers throughout the integration process, avoiding the risk of isolation. It is not, of course, a perfect solution – Sweden, too, is experiencing great political tensions over immigration – but it is undoubtedly one of the most advanced systems, which has made it possible to receive a huge number of refugees, while limiting the social impact on local communities.

It is unclear how the UK should approach the question of migration from within the EU. We will have to see what political choices the UK government makes. I have had the opportunity, as a member of the Italian government, to directly follow this part of the Brexit talks. I have to say that, up to now, the signals sent out by the government have aroused many doubts and concerns in European communities. However, in an effort to be optimistic, I can only recognise that the agreement reached on the status of EU citizens is almost satisfactory.

Prime minister Theresa May has always said that the UK is leaving the EU, but it is not leaving Europe. It is quite clear that such a declaration presupposes a willingness to build up a special relationship not only with European governments and with Brussels institutions, but above all with European citizens living in the United Kingdom. Whatever the outcome of the ongoing negotiations, I hope that respect for European citizens will never fail in British communities. It is up to men and women engaged in politics to find solutions to achieve this purpose.

12 | THE BREXIT GENERATION

Jennifer Jackson-Preece

The first generation to come of age after Brexit are the demographic which wanted Brexit the least. Policymakers should expect this globalised generation to resist any efforts to cut them off from the world. But there are issues which can bring young and old together, and these must be the focus after Brexit.

Brexit has revealed and consolidated a deep cleavage in British politics, now styled as leave versus remain. This divide is about much more than whether or not the United Kingdom should be a member of the European Union. It reflects core differences in values and policy preferences that strongly correlate with age and education.[1] These two characteristics are not unrelated. More than two thirds of voters aged 35 and under possess A-levels or higher qualifications, while fewer than half of those amongst the over 50s can say the same.[2]

The Brexit gap is most striking when we compare the voting behaviour of the youngest and the oldest voters. In the 2016 EU referendum, 73 per cent of young people (under 25s) voted to remain in the European Union, while 60 per cent of old age pensioners (over 65s) voted to leave the European Union.[3] Similarly, in the 2017 UK general election, Labour was forty seven percentage points ahead amongst first time voters (aged 18 and 19), while the Conservatives led by fifty percentage points amongst the oldest voters (aged over 70).[4]

This demographic division is a worrying development, and policy makers on the left should give it their serious attention. A divided society is one characterised by distrust and dislike between groups. Already, leavers and remainers are each more likely to describe the other as "hypocritical", "selfish", and "closed-minded", and their own group as "honest", "intelligent", and "open-minded".[5] When such deep cleavages persist, politics tends to become more combative, more inclined to favour special interests over and above the common good, and less likely to compromise between competing positions. As other commentators have already noted, such divisive identity politics tend to benefit the right more than the left.[6]

Accordingly, the left urgently needs to build bridges across these Brexit divisions, and help citizens find a common ground from which a progressive agenda can be pursued. In order to do that, it must first understand what different groups in society want from Brexit. With that goal in mind, this essay will focus specifically on the generational divide. What do young people think about Brexit, and what are their priorities for the future?

'Generation Brexit'

It is impossible to understand the first generation to come of age after Brexit without recognising that this was the demographic which wanted Brexit the least. A large majority of young people saw their future inside the European Union, and many continue to fight against Brexit. For the most aggrieved, Brexit is something imposed upon them by an older generation who will not have to live with its consequences.

Any effort to bridge the Brexit gap between generations must start from this realisation. And it should acknowledge that for some young people at least, the age demographics of the 2016 referendum constitute a grave injustice. It is only by recognising such grievances, and taking them seriously, that we can begin to build a post-Brexit consensus.

Since the 2016 referendum, there have been several efforts to find out what young people think about Brexit, and what their priorities are for post-Brexit Britain.[7] These efforts have revealed clear and remarkably consistent youth views.

On the whole, young people think the future after Brexit looks bleak.[8] Most young people believe that they will have fewer opportunities, and be financially less well off, as a result of Brexit.[9] They resent the fact that work and study opportunities previously enjoyed by older generations – for example, the ERASMUS scheme – may no longer be available to them.[10]

Young people are less concerned about immigration and less likely to view greater control over immigration after Brexit as justification for reduced employment or educational opportunities.[11] Most young people recognise that immigration brings important advantages, not least by bringing new young people into the work force to help shoulder the tax burden that comes with an aging population.[12] Even that minority of young people who support leave want a softer Brexit that retains opportunities to live, work and study abroad.[13]

Young people generally do not like the social policies associated with the 'leave' position. They worry that leaving the European Union, and its various regulations, will lead to lower standards, particularly in policy areas such as education, the environment, equal rights and social benefits.[14] They want more, not less, investment in schools, universities, the NHS, housing, and environmental protection.[15] They do not believe Brexit campaign promises that money previously sent to Brussels will be re-directed to these areas after Brexit. Instead, many young people fear that Brexit will lead to government spending cuts and reduced services.

Finally, young people reject, often passionately, the nationalism and racism that is associated, rightly or wrongly, with Brexit. They value diversity, and they want Britain to remain a multicultural, inclusive and rights-based society after Brexit.[16]

In sum, young people are not interested in 'taking back control' from Brussels, but they do want to 'take back control' of their own futures. They are deeply unhappy with the public debate on Brexit, both before and after the EU referendum. The perception that youth views have been and continue to be 'ignored' is widespread.[17]

Many young people question the legitimacy of the 2016 referendum, a result they believe was based on misinformation and social media manipulation. Perhaps for this reason, a majority of young people also support a second referendum on the final terms of Brexit.[18] If a second Brexit vote was held, an even bigger majority of 18–24 year olds would vote remain (82 per cent in 2018, up from 73 per cent in 2016), while only 18 per cent would vote leave.[19]

The first globalised generation?

Why do young peoples' views on Brexit differ so much from those of older voters? This is an important question, and one that policy makers on the left should aim to understand.

One reason, as has already been pointed out, is that today's young people are better educated than previous cohorts. And, irrespective of age, greater education increases the likelihood of support for remain.[20]

Another reason is that younger voters possess stronger 'European identities' and 'weaker' national identities as compared to older cohorts. The British Youth Council, for example, found that 62 per cent of young people in the UK feel part of Europe.[21] In contrast, those aged over 50 possess much stronger 'national identities' and very weak 'European identities'.[22] Unsurprisingly, those with stronger 'European identities' were far more likely to vote remain than those with weaker 'European identities.'

More fundamentally, it is claimed that the leave vs. remain cleavage is, at its root, a difference of worldview. In this framing, leavers are the so called 'losers of globalisation,'[23] the people from 'somewhere',[24] only truly at home in a specific national cultural space. In contrast, remainers are the 'winners of globalisation', the people from 'anywhere', who are happy to live in globalised spaces wherever they might be.

If this is true, then the first post-Brexit generation are perhaps best understood as the first truly 'globalised' generation: at home in a diverse and multicultural context, educated, mobile, environmentally aware, socially conscious, and, perhaps, increasingly politically active. The election of 2017 may not have been the 'youthquake' that was initially reported[25] – but the number of young people who have been active in public debate on Brexit is impressive. For example, the Undivided campaign reached 4.4 million young people online.[26]

Going forward, policymakers on the left should expect this globalised generation to resist any and all efforts to cut them off from the world, which is how they tend to regard Brexit. They want to be more closely connected to each other, to Europe and to the rest of the globe.

For this reason, it would be short sighted to assume that the question of Britain's membership of the European Union was fully or finally settled by the 2016 referendum. Even after Brexit, the future relationship between the UK and the EU will likely remain contested for the foreseeable future. The 2016 result could be revisited at some future date, perhaps with a very different outcome, when the first post-Brexit generation comes into power.

But even though young people tend to regard themselves as 'global citizens', this does not make them 'citizens of nowhere'.[27] Young people want more and greater opportunities, for others as well as themselves, at home and abroad. And they are especially committed to progressive measures in respect of inequality, education and the environment.

Building bridges between generations

To begin building bridges between generations, policymakers on the left should make every effort to listen to what young people have to say on Brexit and other issues that matter to them. And those in positions of power should be prepared to act on these suggestions.

If they do, policy makers on the left will find much common ground between themselves and the youngest voters – a commitment to greater equality, a deep respect for diversity, a desire for an inclusive and active democracy, a belief in the value of public services, and the conviction that sustainable development and international cooperation are essential for the future. This is why young people are far more likely to vote Labour than Conservative.

Older generations may be hesitant to embrace the multicultural and globalised future sought by their grandchildren. But many will share young people's desire for greater public spending on public services. A dislike of austerity measures and a commitment to the NHS could become a common rallying cry.

By the same token, a shared dissatisfaction with the Brexit debate may itself create opportunities for a common position. For example, old and young alike are increasingly sceptical about the role of social media in politics. Both may support proposals for regulation of platforms like Facebook, including more stringent protection of personal data.

Conclusion

The deep divisions between leave and remain that have come to separate many young and old voters in Britain today will not disappear over night. There are fundamentally different world views at stake in these debates. And there is little likelihood of a middle ground emerging anytime soon in respect of European Union membership, immigration or multiculturalism.

But there is a possibility for both young and old to come together in defence of public services like the NHS and better protection of personal data online. Policy makers on the left have a responsibility to encourage such generational rapprochements. By building on specific issues like these, we might begin to move towards a progressive partnership between old and young that can begin to heal those divisions exacerbated by Brexit.

---

1 *Financial Times* (2017), 'The six tribes of brexit', www.ft.com/content/61c12868-b350-11e7-a398-73d59db9e399
2 Intergenerational Foundation (October 2017), *Generation Remain* p.19.
3 Lord Ashcroft Polls (2016), "How the United Kingdom voted and why", https://lordashcroftpolls.com/2016/06/how-the-united-kingdom-voted-and-why/
4 YouGov (2017), "How Britain voted at the 2017 general election", https://yougov.co.uk/news/2017/06/13/how-britain-voted-2017-general-election/
5 Sara B. Hobolt, Thomas Leeper and James Tilly (2018), 'Emerging brexit identities' in *Brexit and Public Opinion*, http://ukandeu.ac.uk/wp-content/uploads/2018/01/Public-Opinion.pdf, p.20.
6 Sheri Berman in the *Guardian* (2018), 'Why identity politics benefits the right more than the left', www.theguardian.com/commentisfree/2018/jul/14/identity-politics-right-left-trump-racism

7 See, for example, the activities and reports by the APPG on a Better Brexit for Young People, the British Council, the British Youth Council, Common Vision, Generation Brexit, the Intergenerational Foundation, MyLifeMySay, and Undivided.

8 British Youth Council (July 2017), *The UK Young Ambassadors: Enabling all young people to engage in an Inclusive, diverse and Well-Connected Europe*, pp.7–8.

9 Recent surveys suggest that overall 53 per cent of young people believe that economic prospects after Brexit will be worse (see BBC (2018) 'How young and old would vote on Brexit now', www.bbc.co.uk/news/uk-politics-45098550), with this figure rising to 70 per cent amongst undergraduates (see the *Independent* (2018), 'Final Say: More than 1.4 additional young people could vote in a new Brexit referendum', www.independent.co.uk/news/uk/politics/final-say-brexit-latest-young-voters-second-referendum-remain-poll-a8467631.html).

10 LSE/MLMS For the APPG Better Brexit for Young People (October 2017), *UK Youth Perspectives and priorities for Brexit negotiations*.

11 Common Vision (July 2018), *A Generation Together*, pp.27–28.

12 BBC (2018) 'How young and old would vote on Brexit now', www.bbc.co.uk/news/uk-politics-45098550

13 Undivided (April 2017), *Youth Manifesto Report*.

14 Undivided (April 2017), *Youth manifesto Report*.

15 LSE / MLMS For the APPG Better Brexit for Young People (October 2017), *UK Youth Perspectives and priorities for Brexit negotiations*.

16 Common Vision (July 2018), *A Generation Together*, p.18.

17 See, for example, recurring views expressed by young people on the Generation Brexit platform, https://generationbrexit.org/

18 BBC (2018) 'How young and old would vote on Brexit now', www.bbc.co.uk/news/uk-politics-45098550

19 BBC (2018) 'How young and old would vote on Brexit now', www.bbc.co.uk/news/uk-politics-45098550

20 Intergenerational Foundation, *Generation Remain* (October 2017), p.19.

21 British Youth Council (July 2017), *The UK Young Ambassadors: Enabling all young people to engage in an Inclusive, diverse and Well-Connected Europe*, p.12.

22 Intergenerational Foundation, *Generation Remain* (October 2017), p.19.

23 Sara Hobolt (2016), 'Voters have Punished the Elite and This is Not Just a British Phenomenon', http://blogs.lse.ac.uk/brexit/2016/06/24/voters-have-punished-the-elite-and-this-is-not-just-a-british-phenomenon/

24 David Goodhart (2017) 'Anywheres vs. Somewheres: The split that made Brexit inevitable', www.newstatesman.com/politics/uk/2017/03/anywheres-vs-somewheres-split-made-brexit-inevitable

25 BBC News (2018), 'The myth of the 2017 'youthquake' election, www.bbc.co.uk/news/uk-politics-42747342

26 Common Vision (July 2018), *A Generation Together*, p.70.

27 Joe Porter, in the *Guardian* (2016), 'Brexit will affect the young more than the anyone. Heed our voices', www.theguardian.com/commentisfree/2016/dec/09/brexit-young-people-undivided-campaign

13 | EU PERSPECTIVE
FACING UP TO THE
GENERATIONAL DIVIDE
Kaisa Penny

Politicians across the EU must do more to bridge the generational divide. The EU is already a significant actor on issues that affect young people, but it must do more to hear their concerns.

The majority of young people in the UK voted to remain in the European Union.[1] The proportion of those wanting to leave the European Union grew with every generation. Bridging this generational gap will be a critical challenge for British politicians over the coming decades.

But it is not the British alone who have such a gap. The yearly data collected by the Eurobarometer surveys shows that the concerns and interests of Europeans often vary more between the generations than between nationalities. Young people are, for example, more concerned than older generations about climate change, changing labour markets, fake news and extremism.

The picture painted by these surveys and other research shows that young people are more concerned with issues that require cross border cooperation. They also show that young people are more positive about the European Union. According to the Eurobarometer survey in spring 2018, 60 per cent of EU citizens feel positive about the

EU membership of their home country. This number was 67 per cent for the respondents who were under 25 and 56 per cent for those over 55. Young Europeans are both more supportive of the single currency (67 per cent to 58 per cent of over 55s) and possible further enlargement of the Union (64 per cent to 35 per cent).[2] Young people are also more likely to think that there should be more decision making at the European level on health care and social security issues and would like to see harmonised welfare provision.[3]

At the same time as younger generations look more favourably towards Europe, more than half of all Europeans believe that life will be more difficult for the children of today than it was for themselves and previous generations.[4] This reveals the challenge that European societies face. Ever since the creation of welfare states in Europe, the belief has been that development and growth will make it easier for each generation, and that we will increase prosperity for all. Now, for the first time, we are in a situation where this is no longer the expectation – and the priorities and concerns of the generations are increasingly divided.

Young people haven't been missing from the EU's agenda. During the economic crisis the issue of youth unemployment and mass migration of young people from the so-called crisis countries raised a lot of debate and also policy solutions. But mass youth unemployment has brought to light the frustration and distrust young people have towards the political system. This was best seen in the Occupy and Indignados movements, and through an increase in demonstrations. But we've also seen passivism, hopelessness and support for extremist movements. The far-right and populist movements have gained momentum.

It is time to face the challenge of this generational divide. It will not be an easy task, especially considering the fragmentation of the political landscape. But it is a necessary one in order to maintain the coherence of our societies and, in the longer term, support for the social contract which binds our welfare states together.

The European Union has tools available for this challenge, and can do more to act on the issues which concern young people. The Union is a significant actor on the global level on migration, climate change and combatting the spread of fake news. It also has an increasing budget for education, research and the mobility of young people. The EU has already agreed upon the principle and method of addressing the youth unemployment crisis through the youth guarantee – and now it must simply deliver.

With all the pre-existing possibilities, good progress can be made if there is political will. But there are also significant issues with representation and a lack of dialogue with young people which result in a democratic deficit and feed the generational divide. As we move into a new era both in the UK and in the European Union, politicians must do more to hear young people as well as to act in their interests.

---

1 https://lordashcroftpolls.com/2016/06/how-the-united-kingdom-voted-and-why/
2 Standard Eurobarometer 89 (2018).
3 Special Eurobarometer 467 (2017).
4 Special Eurobarometer 467 (2017).

14 | REJOINERS?

Stephen Bush

British pro-Europeans can feel confident that the UK will seek to return to the EU at some point in the future. The economic imperative won't change and such pressures always triumph over political forces. But it is less likely we'll see the political leadership required to make the UK's second stay in the EU more stable.

It is a little past midnight on Thursday 3 June 2032. Newcastle is the first counting area to declare, and the result is overwhelming: by 40 points, the people of Newcastle have voted to rejoin the European Union. Minutes later, Sunderland follows suit, by a smaller but still crushing majority, with 'rejoin' triumphing over 'remain' (out of the EU) by 15 points.

"An old dawn has broken, has it not?" a 79-year-old Tony Blair triumphantly tweets. By the early hours of Friday, it is clear: the people of the United Kingdom of England and Wales (UKEW) have voted by an overwhelming margin to become the European Union's 35th member. The value of sterling climbs to a decade high of 59 cents to a pound while, on the Scottish border, residents of the border towns dance outside checkpoints separating England from its neighbour. Property prices along the border shoot up in anticipation of the trading bonanza that is expected to arrive once the two nations are once again in the same

market and customs area. The first European country to welcome UKEW back into the fold is not Scotland but Ireland, though analysts suggest that the Taoiseach's real agenda is to guarantee English support in the coming talks with unionist paramilitaries.

Although many of the bloc's creditor nations are reluctant to add another net recipient to the EU, after UKEW agrees to a series of tough financial promises to balance the books and get the country's pension liabilities under control, UKEW is welcomed back if not with open arms but with at least a warm handshake. On 1 January 2034, the United Kingdom of England and Wales is welcomed back into the European Union.

Farfetched? The circumstances – and the scale of the endorsement for re-joining the European Union – are deliberately provocative. Prediction is a mug's game, but the odds that British public opinion will shift in favour of remaining in the European Union – if, indeed, it hasn't already – are extremely high. The Brexit vote was driven not by economics but, in the main, by culture – and the cultural mores that inclined people towards a remain vote are more widely represented among the young than the old. Pro-remain politicians and celebrities should stop talking about the fact that most Brexit voters will be dead soon, because it is highly unattractive and extremely counterproductive. But it is, nonetheless, true that anyone who wants us to rejoin the European Union can, in the long term, get away with their highly unattractive language about leave voters, their embarrassing hashtags and their sub-par leadership, because time is on pro-Europeans' side. Tomorrow belongs to them, no matter how little they do to deserve it.

It is the Brexiteers who must desperately remove the taint of culture war from Britain's leave vote if the United Kingdom's time out of the European Union is to be anything other than a ten-year proposition. It could be that once Brexit is secured, enough of the leave establishment will be able to turn its mind to winning over remainers to futureproof Brexit – but it doesn't feel particularly likely.

No amount of careful wooing of public opinion can change the fundamental challenges of Brexit, all of which make it more likely than not that support for leaving the European Union will decline, rather than rise.

The 2016 referendum was, at its core, a decision about how best to maximise British sovereignty. British voters opted, albeit by a narrow margin, to choose political freedom over economic freedom. Of course, as the left has always known, the freedom of the poor is a pretty poor version of freedom: yes, you have more theoretical freedom, but you can't take advantage of it when you're broke.

The biggest long-run force working against Brexit is that voters in general – whether they backed remain, leave, or simply stayed at home in 2016 – are always less willing to absorb economic losses than they think they are. Voters re-elected a Conservative government promising £12bn worth of welfare cuts in 2015, and immediately revolted when that government actually tried to make anything close to £12bn worth of welfare cuts. The economic costs of Brexit will be no different. A soft Brexit which does not maximise British sovereignity but instead maintains the current rate of trade might be more politically enduring outside Westminster, but it lacks sufficient support in parliament. The only available political exit, as long as the Conservatives are in office, will be a hard one. And that Brexit will be no more popular than cuts to tax credits were.

That the bulk of the Labour party membership continue to be pro-European and select pro-Europeans in parliamentary constituencies means that, if there is a Labour government (whether in majority or some form of coalition) again, the chances are high that, at the least, a significant chunk of backbenchers will want to re-open the question. And if public opinion moves, other Labour politicians won't want to stand in the way.

So the bigger question is not "could British voters decide they are better off inside the European Union?" but: what will the European Union look like? Will be it an organisation that wants the United Kingdom in it? What might a stable and sustainable British membership look like? And will the European Union even survive?

Let's take that last question first: will the European Union still be around in 20 or 30 years? Don't forget that the United Kingdom is by no means the only European nation to have seen political upheaval and crisis over the last decade, and the problems all have the same roots: the global financial crisis and the migrant crisis, both of which have destabilised European politics. The movement of people from the global south to Europe has been driven by a variety of forces: political collapse and war caused by the Arab Spring and economic migration caused by climate change. But it has already caused significant increases in support for the nativist right across the continent and was a factor behind the United Kingdom's leave vote. It also helped boost support for the far right in Germany, Austria and Italy.

The bad news is that the movement of people before the referendum is nothing compared to the far bigger movements that will be triggered by the Earth's changing climate. There is no compelling reason to suppose that the European Union will survive a greater and deeper migrant crisis.

That's the worst case scenario. The good news is that there is little point worrying about it. If it happens, the result, both in terms of what it means for the rest of the European Union and for the United Kingdom – whatever shape it may be – is too bad to ameliorate.

Let's instead look at a future where the European Union survives. What might re-entry look like in that world?

The European Union will of course continue to grow and change after Brexit and its evolution will be different because of the departure of the United Kingdom. So what might the European Union come to look like?

One of the significant differences is that all of the bloc's power players, by any metric you care to name (significance of contribution to the EU's budget, number of votes held via qualified majority voting, presence in the bureaucratic structures of the bloc), will all be members of the Eurozone. One of the pressures exerted on the United Kingdom's membership of the European Union was that neither British politics nor economics made it achievable or desirable for the country to be a member of the Euro. But outside the single currency, the United Kingdom was an increasingly less significant player in the internal politics of the bloc.

Much was made during the referendum campaign of the idea that the United Kingdom had been sold a false bill of goods: a common market, not a federal project. The truth is that the European project was always a political project as well as an economic one, and was clearly advertised as such when the United Kingdom joined. The real false promise was that membership of the European Community would allow the United Kingdom to regain its status as a power player on the world stage. While it was a German politician – Konrad Adenauer – speaking to a French one – his opposite number Guy Mollet – who said that "Europe will be our revenge" against the rising power of the United States, it was a line believed by British politicians more than anyone else.

But the United Kingdom is not a power player on the world stage, though it has been one within the European Union. Staying outside the Eurozone didn't end that but it did reduce it. Any union the United Kingdom rejoined would be one in which the Eurozone was still more influential and the countries outside the monetary union less so. That would be doubly the case for Britain if it maintained its Cameron-era position of being not only outside the monetary union but being the only member state not to opt in to at least some of the Eurozone-wide measures.

It is unlikely that Emmanuel Macron's proposals will ever be implemented in full. It requires not only for him to remain in office, but to be blessed with a German Chancellor and a Dutch Prime Minister who are not only sympathetic to his reforms but have the political strength to deliver them at home, which is almost certainly not going to happen. If they did, the United Kingdom would be re-joining the bloc in a subordinate position. The false promise of the 1970s, that the United Kingdom could keep its great power pretensions through the European Community, would have to be faced off once and for all.

The same would be true for the United Kingdom's prized opt-outs. As it stands, the reality is that the United Kingdom is already less special than its political class likes to pretend. Yes, the United Kingdom has more opt-outs – four – than any other member state. It has an opt-out from joining the European single currency, from being part of the Schengen Agreement, on security and justice measures, and on aspects of the Charter of Fundamental rights. But it shares all of its opt-outs with another member state: Denmark in the case of the single currency, defence and security matters, Ireland over Schengen, and Poland over the Charter of Fundamental Rights. Its opt-out from the Charter of Fundamental Rights means very little in practice and its opt-out from joining the single currency means even less. Most countries that are not already in the Eurozone are joining it only in the same sense that Turkey is joining the European Union: it will happen shortly after the heat death of the universe.

As for security, the United Kingdom's opt-outs are weaker than Denmark's and are more significant for past measures than they will be to future ones.

What about Schengen? Well, in practice, entering Schengen would be an unalloyed positive for the United Kingdom: as an island nation the country would still have considerable protections of its borders but it would open up the possibility of train travel across the continent that extended beyond London and into the country's other great cities. But crucially, what guarantees the UK's Schengen opt-out is that Ireland, which shares a land border with the UK, currently has one too.

But, frankly, the United Kingdom would be better off economically within Schengen and it will only be able to become a stable member of the European Union when its political class has the stomach to argue that. It will also require an acceptance that the United Kingdom will be a less significant member of the bloc than it was on 23 June 2016. And on current evidence, anyone hoping for that will be in for a long wait.

But, despite that, British pro-Europeans can feel comfortable in expecting that the United Kingdom will seek to return to the bloc at some point in the future. The economic imperative won't change and in the long term, economic pressures triumph over political forces. But the political leadership required to make the United Kingdom's second stay within the European Union more stable and enduring than the first looks likely to remain in short supply.

The left's agenda for the UK and EU

EDITED BY
Olivia Bailey

FOREWORD BY
Keir Starmer QC MP

FABIAN SOCIETY

Discussion Guide: Beyond Brexit

How to use this discussion guide

The guide can be used in various ways by Fabian local societies, local political party meetings and trade union branches, student societies, NGOs and other groups.

- You might hold a discussion among local members or invite a guest speaker – for example, an MP, academic or local practitioner to lead a group discussion.

- Some different key themes are suggested. You might choose to spend 15–20 minutes on each area, or decide to focus the whole discussion on one of the issues for a more detailed discussion.

A discussion could address one or more of the following questions:

1. What should the future relationship between the EU and UK look like? How can progressives best make the case for a close working relationship after Brexit?

2. What is the future of defence and security cooperation? And how can Britain step up its role on the world stage after Brexit?

3. How can progressives counter the rise of right wing nationalism?

4. What is a left agenda for responding to concerns about immigration? And how can we encourage better social cohesion?

5. How can we start to bridge the divides that the Brexit vote revealed?

6. What should be part of a progressive agenda to deal with the economic drivers of Brexit?

Please let us know what you think

Whatever view you take of the issues, we would very much like to hear about your discussion. Please send us a summary of your debate (perhaps 300 words) to info@fabians.org.uk

---